GCSE Physics

Set A Paper 1
Higher Tier

In addition to this paper you should have:
- A ruler.
- A calculator.

Centre name				
Centre number				
Candidate number				

Time allowed:
- 1 hour 45 minutes

Surname	
Other names	
Candidate signature	

Instructions to candidates
- Write your name and other details in the spaces provided above.
- Answer **all** questions in the spaces provided.
- Do all rough work on the paper.
- Cross out any work you do not want to be marked.

Information for candidates
- The marks available are given in brackets at the end of each question.
- There are 100 marks available for this paper.
- You are allowed to use a calculator.
- You should use good English and present your answers in a clear and organised way.
- For Questions 4.2, 6.4 and 8.4 ensure that your answers have a clear and logical structure, include the right scientific terms, spelt correctly, and include detailed, relevant information.

For examiner's use

Q	Attempt Nº 1	2	3	Q	Attempt Nº 1	2	3
1				7			
2				8			
3				9			
4				10			
5				11			
6							
				Total			

Advice to candidates
- In calculations show clearly how you worked out your answers.
- An equation sheet is included at the back of this paper.

Answer all questions in the spaces provided

1 A student is investigating how the current through a resistor varies with potential difference.

During the experiment, the student makes sure that the resistor remains at a constant temperature.

1.1 Explain why it is important that the resistor is kept at a constant temperature.

....

....
[1 mark]

1.2 Suggest how the student could have kept the temperature of the resistor constant during the experiment.

....

....
[1 mark]

Figure 1 shows a graph of the student's results.

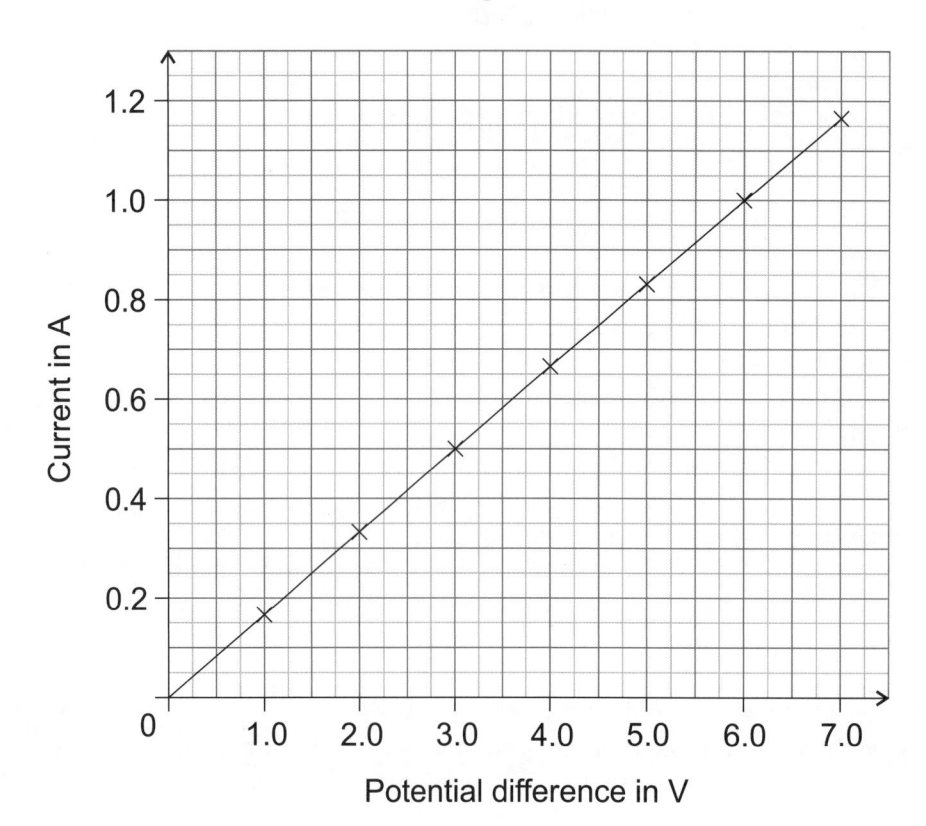

Figure 1

1.3 State the equation that links potential difference, current and resistance.

....
[1 mark]

1.4 Using **Figure 1**, calculate the resistance of the resistor.

....

....

....

Resistance = ... Ω
[2 marks]

1.5 Which of the following statements is a correct conclusion that can be drawn from the graph in **Figure 1**?
Tick **one** box.

☐ The resistor is ohmic because the graph is linear.

☐ The resistor is non-ohmic because the graph is linear.

☐ It is not possible to tell if the resistor is ohmic or non-ohmic from the graph.
[1 mark]

1.6 The student repeats their experiment using a diode instead of a resistor.
On the axes below, sketch the graph you would expect the student to obtain for a diode connected in the forward direction.

[axes: Current in A (vertical) vs Potential difference in V (horizontal)]

[1 mark]

Turn over for the next question

2 A group of people are pushing a broken down car.
They got the car to start moving by pushing the car from a stationary position.

2.1 Describe the main energy transfer that occurs when the people push the car to start it moving.

....

....
[2 marks]

The group push the car up a hill. **Figure 2** shows the position of the car on the hill after it has been pushed, in comparison to its starting point.

Figure 2

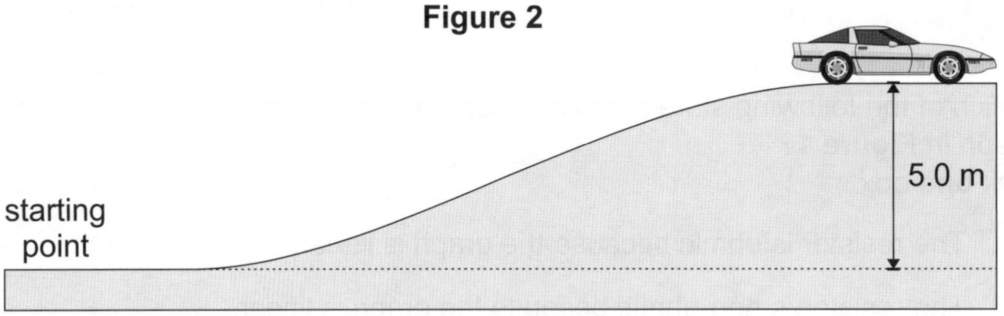

5.0 m

starting point

The car has a mass of 1200 kg. The gravitational field strength is 9.8 N/kg.

2.2 Write down the equation that links gravitational potential energy, mass, gravitational field strength and height.

....
[1 mark]

2.3 Calculate the energy transferred to the car's gravitational potential energy store as it climbed the hill.

....

....

Energy = ... J
[2 marks]

107 000 J of energy was transferred by the people to the car as they pushed it up the hill.

2.4 Suggest **one** way in which energy may have been wasted when the car was pushed up the hill.

....
[1 mark]

Leave blank

3 The UK mains supply of electricity is an alternating potential difference with a size of around 230 V.

3.1 Describe the difference between an alternating potential difference and a direct potential difference.

....

....

....

[2 marks]

Figure 3 shows an electrical appliance that connects to the mains supply. It is connected to the mains using a three-core cable containing a live wire, an earth wire and a neutral wire.

Figure 3

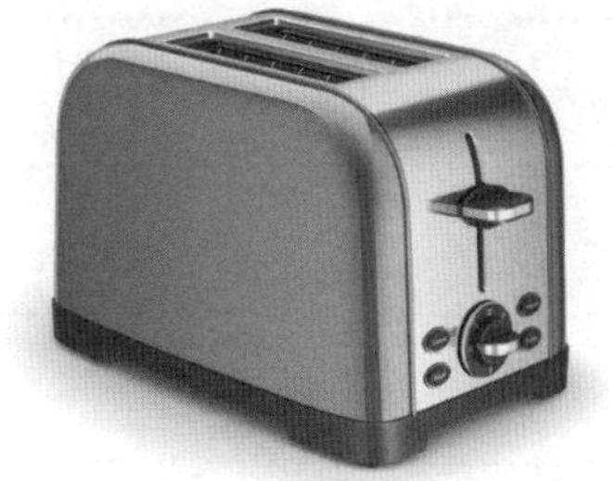

3.2 State the potential difference between the live wire and the earth wire.

....

[1 mark]

3.3 Explain why a connection between the live wire and the earth wire can be dangerous.

....

....

....

....

....

[2 marks]

Question 3 continues on the next page

Turn over ▶

Mains electricity is transmitted around the country through the national grid.

3.4 Describe what is meant by the national grid.

....

....
[1 mark]

3.5 Explain why electricity is transmitted through the national grid at a potential difference that is much greater than 230 V.

....

....

....

....

....

....

....
[3 marks]

3.6 Mains electricity is supplied to consumers at around 230 V.
Name the device that is used to decrease the potential difference of the electricity supply carried by the national grid to around 230 V.

....
[1 mark]

4 Some students are investigating different radioactive sources.
Their teacher gives them 3 sources: source X, source Y and source Z.
The teacher tells them that one emits only alpha radiation, one emits only beta radiation, and one emits only gamma radiation.

4.1 Gamma radiation is an electromagnetic wave.
State the part of an atom that gamma radiation is emitted from.

....
[1 mark]

The teacher provides the students with some equipment, shown in **Figure 4**.

Figure 4

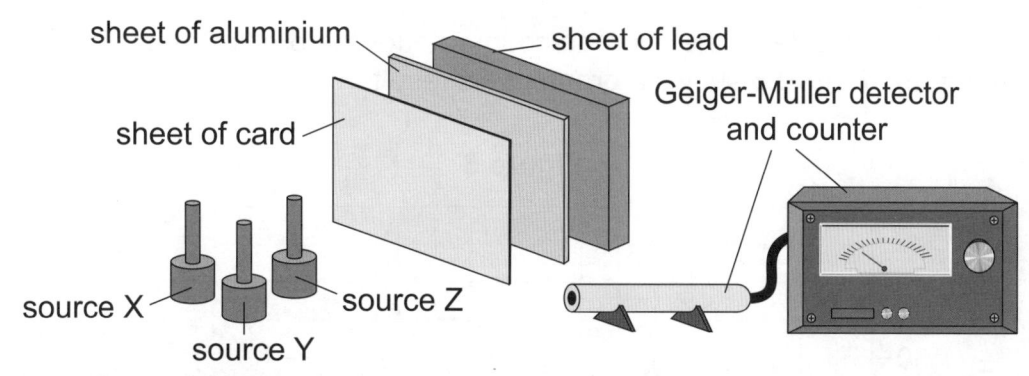

4.2 Describe an experiment that the students could carry out using the equipment in **Figure 4** to determine which type of radiation each source emits.

[6 marks]

Question 4 continues on the next page

Turn over ▶

As a safety precaution, the students are told they always need to use tongs to pick up the radioactive sources.

4.3 Explain how this precaution helps to keep the students safe as they do the experiment.

....

....
[1 mark]

The teacher uses another Geiger-Müller detector and counter to measure the radiation in the classroom throughout a normal school day.

Every hour, he calculates the average count rate for the previous hour in counts per minute (cpm). **Figure 5** shows a graph of his results.

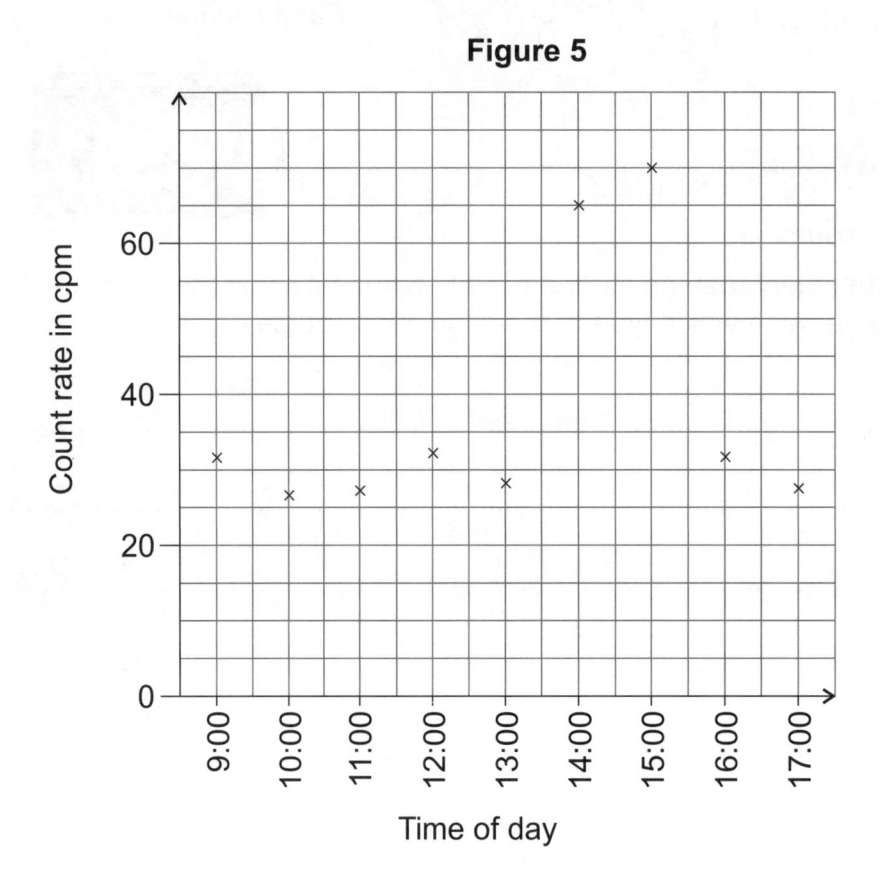

Figure 5

4.4 Suggest why the count rate is much higher at 14:00 and 15:00 than at any other time during the day.

....

....
[1 mark]

4.5 Draw a line on **Figure 5** to show the average count rate due to background radiation.
[1 mark]

A student at another school sees the graph in **Figure 5**.

He measures an average count rate of 50 cps in his science classroom when no radioactive sources are being used.
He concludes that there must be an exposed radioactive source somewhere in the classroom.

4.6 Comment on the student's conclusion.

....

....
[1 mark]

Cosmic rays are a natural source of background radiation.

4.7 State **two** other sources of background radiation.

1. ....

2. ....
[2 marks]

Turn over for the next question

5 Table 1 shows some properties of different types of light bulb.

Table 1

Light Bulb Type	Input Power in W	Output Power in W	Lifetime in h
Filament lamp	60.0	12.0	2 000
Compact fluorescent lamp	15.0	3.75	10 000
LED	14.5	12.0	50 000

When the LED bulb listed in **Table 1** is used in a house, a current of 0.063 A passes through the bulb.

5.1 Calculate the resistance of the LED bulb.

Resistance = ... Ω
[2 marks]

5.2 Using the information in **Table 1**, suggest **two** reasons why LEDs are more popular than filament lamps.

1. ....

2. ....

[2 marks]

An older type of filament lamp has an efficiency of 5.0%.

5.3 Calculate the total power input required for this bulb to have the same useful power output as a compact fluorescent bulb.

....

....

....

....

Total power input = ... W

[3 marks]

Turn over for the next question

6 Table 2 shows some examples of radioactive isotopes.

Table 2

Radioactive isotope	Half-life	Main type of radiation emitted
Radon-220	55.6 seconds	Alpha
Americium-241	433 years	Alpha
Phosphorus-32	14 days	Beta
Strontium-90	29 years	Beta
Technetium-99m	6 hours	Gamma
Cobalt-60	5 years	Gamma

6.1 State what is meant by the term isotope.

....

....
[1 mark]

Figure 6 shows a beta particle. A beta particle has the same electric field pattern around it as an isolated charged sphere.

Figure 6

6.2 Complete **Figure 6** by drawing an electric field pattern around the beta particle.
[2 marks]

6.3 Describe how the nucleus of a radon-220 atom changes when it decays.

....

....
[1 mark]

A patient is to be injected with a radioactive isotope to be used as a medical tracer.
The isotope will travel around their body in their bloodstream.
The radiation the isotope emits will be detected outside the body with a detector.

6.4 One of the isotopes in **Table 2** can be used as a medical tracer.
State and explain which isotope is best suited for using as a medical tracer.

....

....

....

....

....

....

....

....

....
[4 marks]

The patient took part in a trial of a new cancer treatment that uses radiation.

6.5 The results of the trial are submitted to an academic journal to be published.
Give **two** reasons why this is important.

1. ....

....

2. ....

....
[2 marks]

Turn over for the next question   **Turn over ▶**

7 A scuba tank contains a fixed mass of air at a high pressure.
The tank contains 3.0 kg of compressed air.
The density of uncompressed air is 1.225 kg/m³.

7.1 Calculate the volume that the air would take up if it were released from the tank.

....

....

Volume = ... m³
[3 marks]

A fire breaks out in the storage room where the scuba tank is kept.
This causes the temperature of the air inside the tank to increase.

7.2 Explain, in terms of the particles, how an increase in temperature affects the pressure of a gas in a container with a fixed volume.

....

....

....

....

....

....
[3 marks]

7.3 Explain why the increase in temperature of the scuba tank can be dangerous.

....

....
[1 mark]

7.4 State and explain how the increase in temperature affects the density of the gas inside the tank.

....

....

....
[2 marks]

8 A student wants to investigate how the resistance of a thermistor changes with temperature. **Figure 7** shows the equipment the student uses to carry out an experiment.

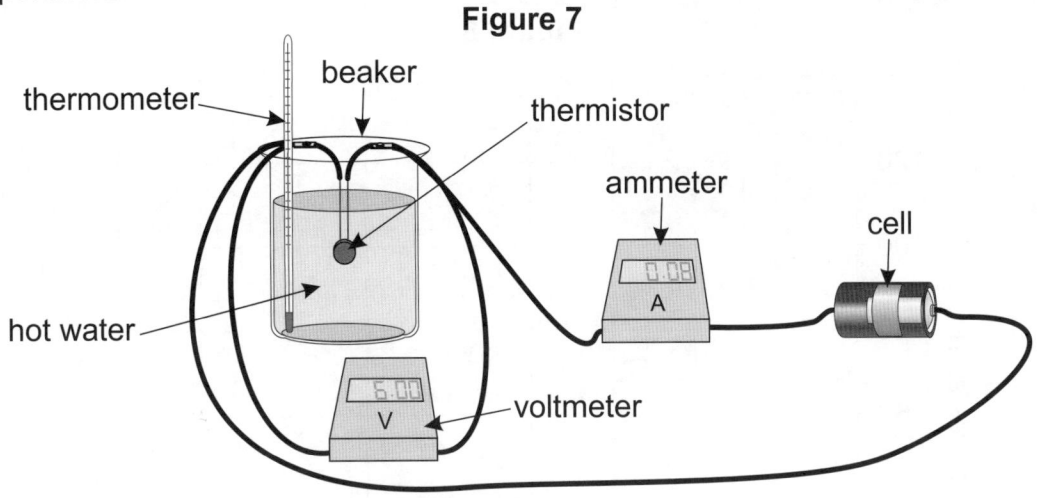

Figure 7

The student carried out the following method:

1. The student filled the beaker with hot water, and placed the thermometer and the thermistor into the water. They waited for the temperature to drop to 80 °C.
2. The student recorded the current in the circuit from the ammeter, and the potential difference across the thermistor from the voltmeter.
3. They calculated the resistance of the thermistor using these measurements and the equation $V = IR$.
4. They repeated steps 2 and 3 every 10 °C as the water cooled.

The student carried out the experiment three times. **Table 3** shows their results.

Table 3

Temperature (°C)	Resistance Trial 1 (Ω)	Resistance Trial 2 (Ω)	Resistance Trial 3 (Ω)	Mean Resistance (Ω)
80	70	70	73	71
70	78	75	75	76
60	83	81	82	82
50	93	89	88	90
40	98	99	103	100
30	120	118	122	120

8.1 Calculate the uncertainty in the mean resistance at 60 °C.

Uncertainty = ± .... Ω
[2 marks]

Question 8 continues on the next page

Turn over ▶

8.2 **Figure 8** shows an incomplete graph of the student's results.
Complete **Figure 8** by plotting the remaining points.
Draw a line of best fit.

Figure 8

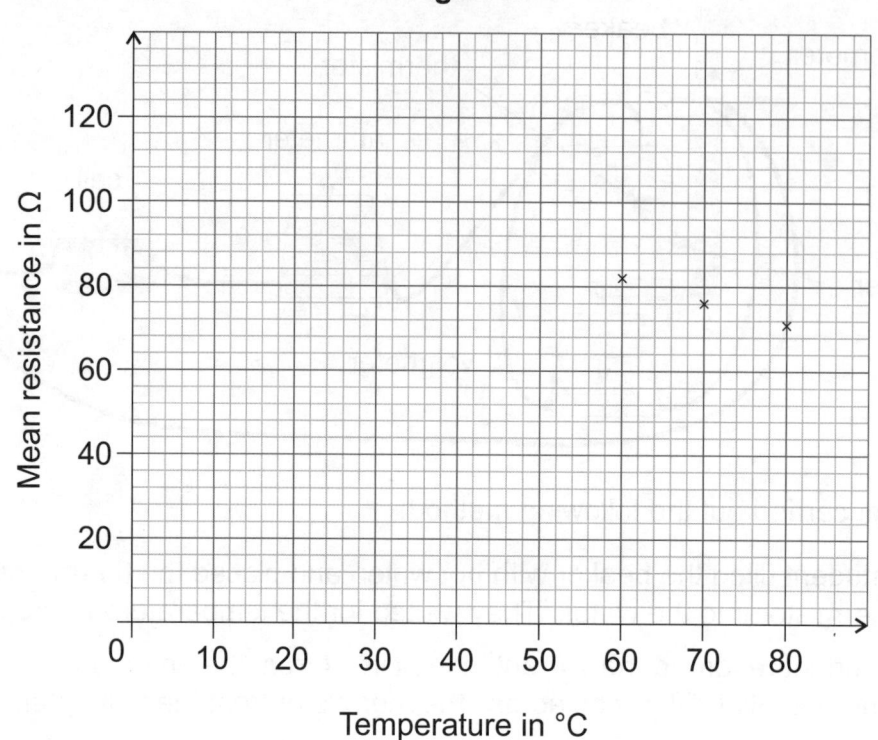

[Graph: Mean resistance in Ω (y-axis, 0 to 120+) vs Temperature in °C (x-axis, 0 to 80). Three points plotted with x marks at approximately (60, 82), (70, 75), (80, 70).]

[3 marks]

8.3 Suggest **two** ways the student could extend the range of their results.

1. ....

   ....

2. ....

   ....

[2 marks]

The student used the thermistor in the circuit shown in **Figure 9**.
They left it in a room for a full 24 hours.
The ammeter was connected to a data-logger, which recorded the current through the circuit every hour.

Figure 9

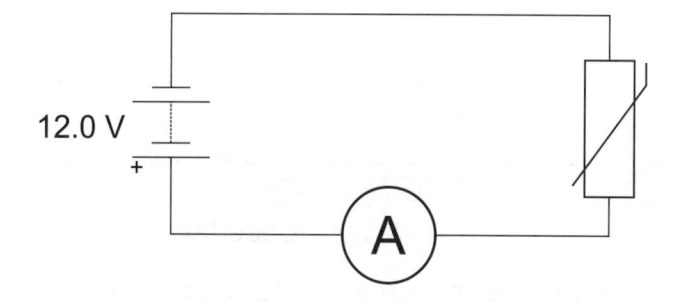

[Circuit diagram showing a 12.0 V battery connected in series with an ammeter (A) and a thermistor.]

Figure 10 shows the graph of the results collected by the data-logger.

Figure 10

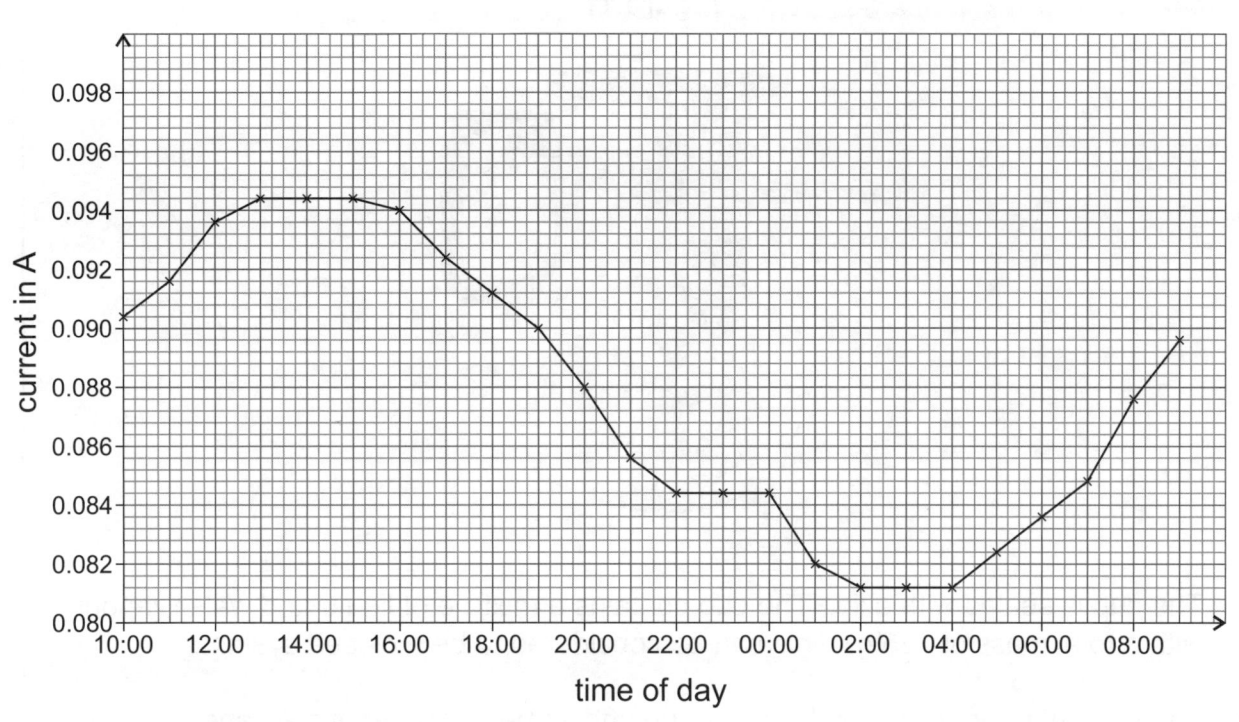

8.4 Using **Figure 10**, describe how the temperature of the room changed during the 24 hour period.

....

....

....

....

....

....

....

....

....

[4 marks]

Turn over for the next question

Turn over ▶

9 A student has a cup of coffee, like the one shown in **Figure 11**.

Figure 11

The cup is sealed with a lid. The cup contains a mixture of liquid and water vapour, with a total mass of 225 g. This can be considered to be a closed system.

The student removes the lid from the cup and some water vapour escapes. He then replaces the lid.

9.1 State and explain how the average energy of the particles of the system has changed after the lid has been removed and replaced.

....

....

....

....

....

....

[2 marks]

All the water vapour that escaped from the cup condenses back into liquid water.
As the water vapour condenses, it releases 20 300 J of energy.
The specific latent heat of vaporisation of water vapour is 2 257 000 J/kg.

9.2 Calculate the total mass inside the cup after the lid is removed and replaced.
Give your answer in grams.

....

....

....

....

....

Mass = ... g
[3 marks]

A cardboard coffee cup is shown in **Figure 12**.
The coffee cup has a thick ring of cardboard around it.
Cardboard has a low thermal conductivity. The cardboard ring helps to reduce the energy transferred to a person's hand when they are holding the cup.

Figure 12

9.3 Explain why you could not consider the coffee in the cardboard cup a closed system.

....

....

....

....
[2 marks]

Turn over for the next question

Turn over ▶

10 A racing car is being prepared for a race.

The engine of the car transfers energy released from burning the fuel to the car's motor to move the car. The engine contains a number of moving parts.

Before a race, the engineers working on the car apply oil to parts of the engine.

10.1 Suggest how applying oil to parts of the engine helps to prevent it from overheating.

....

....

....

....

[2 marks]

During a test drive, the car travels down a straight track at a constant speed. While travelling down this track, the car has 2 400 000 J of energy in its kinetic energy store. The car has a mass of 750 kg.

10.2 Calculate the speed of the car.
Give your answer in km/h.

....

....

....

....

....

....

Speed = ... km/h
[3 marks]

As the car approaches the end of the track, the car brakes and comes to rest.

As it comes to rest, 80% of the energy in the car's kinetic energy store is transferred to the thermal energy stores of the brake discs.

There are four brake discs. Each brake disc has a mass of 1500 g.
The specific heat capacity of the brake discs is 600 J/kg°C.

10.3 Calculate the average rise in temperature of a brake disc as the car comes to rest.

....

....

....

....

....

....

....

Change in temperature = ... °C
[4 marks]

Brake discs can be damaged and fail if they get too hot.

After the test drive, the engineers replace the brake discs with a new set.
They can replace them with an identical set of brake discs, Set A, or a different set, Set B, that are the same size and mass but have a higher specific heat capacity.

10.4 Suggest which set of brake discs the engineers should use.
Justify your answer.

....

....

....

[2 marks]

Turn over for the next question

Turn over ▶

11 A student is using the circuit shown in **Figure 13**.

Figure 13

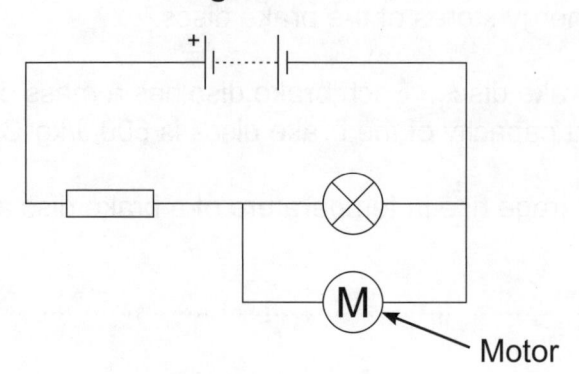

Motor

The potential difference of the battery is 9.0 V.
The potential difference across the resistor is 6.2 V.

The total current through the circuit is 0.40 A.
The current through the filament bulb is 0.15 A.

11.1 Calculate the energy transferred by the motor in 30 s.

....

Energy = ... J
[5 marks]

The student decides to change his circuit. He wants to change it so that either all the components are connected in series, as shown in **Figure 14**, or all the components are connected in parallel, as shown in **Figure 15**.

Figure 14

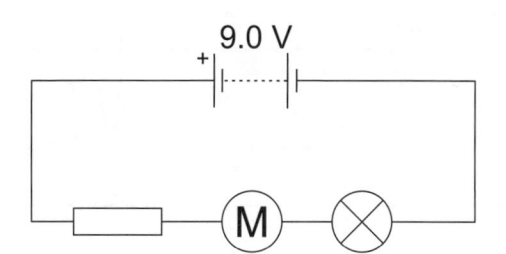

Figure 15

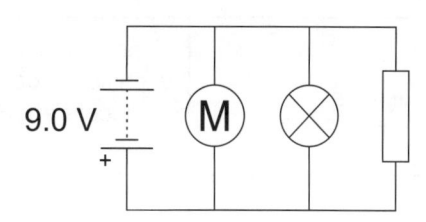

11.2 Explain why the power of the motor is lower in the circuit shown in **Figure 14** than in the circuit shown in **Figure 15**.

....

....

....

....

....

....
[3 marks]

11.3 The student builds the circuit in **Figure 14**.
He increases the potential difference of the power supply.
Explain why this causes the total resistance of the circuit to increase.

....

....
[1 mark]

END OF QUESTIONS

GCSE Physics Equation Sheet

$p = h\rho g$	p pressure due to a column of liquid h height of column ρ density of liquid g gravitational field strength
$v^2 - u^2 = 2as$	v final velocity u initial velocity a acceleration s distance
$F = \dfrac{m\Delta v}{\Delta t}$	F force $m\Delta v$ change in momentum Δt time taken
$E_e = \frac{1}{2}ke^2$	E_e elastic potential energy k spring constant e extension
$\Delta E = mc\Delta\theta$	ΔE change in thermal energy m mass c specific heat capacity $\Delta\theta$ change in temperature
period = $\dfrac{1}{\text{frequency}}$	
magnification = $\dfrac{\text{image height}}{\text{object height}}$	
$F = BIl$	F force on a current-carrying conductor (at right angles to the field) B magnetic flux density I current l length
$E = mL$	E thermal energy for a change of state m mass L specific latent heat
$\dfrac{V_p}{V_s} = \dfrac{n_p}{n_s}$	V_p potential difference across primary coil V_s potential difference across secondary coil n_p number of turns in primary coil n_s number of turns in secondary coil
$V_s I_s = V_p I_p$	V_s potential difference across secondary coil I_s current in secondary coil V_p potential difference across primary coil I_p current in primary coil
For gases: pV = constant	p pressure V volume

GCSE Physics

Set A Paper 2

Higher Tier

In addition to this paper you should have:
- A ruler.
- A calculator.
- A protractor.

Centre name

Centre number

Candidate number

Surname

Other names

Candidate signature

Time allowed:
- 1 hour 45 minutes

Instructions to candidates
- Write your name and other details in the spaces provided above.
- Answer **all** questions in the spaces provided.
- Do all rough work on the paper.
- Cross out any work you do not want to be marked.

Information for candidates
- The marks available are given in brackets at the end of each question.
- There are 100 marks available for this paper.
- You are allowed to use a calculator.
- You should use good English and present your answers in a clear and organised way.
- For Questions 4.6, 7.5 and 9.5 ensure that your answers have a clear and logical structure, include the right scientific terms, spelt correctly, and include detailed, relevant information.

Advice to candidates
- In calculations show clearly how you worked out your answers.
- An equation sheet is included at the back of this paper.

For examiner's use							
Q	Attempt Nº			Q	Attempt Nº		
	1	2	3		1	2	3
1				6			
2				7			
3				8			
4				9			
5				10			
Total							

Answer **all** questions in the spaces provided

1 A group of students investigate how the angle of a ramp affects the final speed of a trolley that rolls down the ramp.

Figure 1 shows the basic set-up the students use.

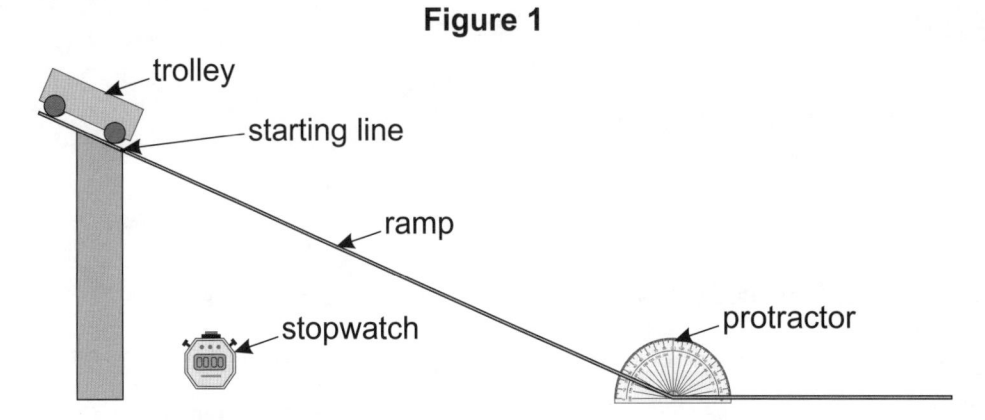

Figure 1

Student 1 carries out the following experiment using 6 different ramps:

1. He sets up the first ramp so it forms a 10° angle with the bench.
2. He measures the distance between the starting line and the bottom of the ramp.
3. He places the trolley at the starting line.
4. He lets go of the trolley and starts the stopwatch.
5. He stops the stopwatch as soon as the trolley reaches the bottom of the ramp, and records the time.
6. He calculates the speed of the trolley using the distance and time measured.
7. He changes the ramp for another ramp. He positions the new ramp so it is 5° steeper than the previous ramp.
8. He then repeats steps 1-7 until he has used each ramp.

1.1 State **two** problems with Student 1's experiment.
In each case, explain how the student could improve their experiment.

1. ....

....

....

2. ....

....

....

[4 marks]

When the ramp is at an angle of 30°, the force pulling the trolley down the ramp is 50% of the trolley's weight. The trolley has a mass of 0.40 kg and the gravitational field strength is 9.8 N/kg.

1.2 Give the equation that links weight, mass and gravitational field strength.

....
[1 mark]

1.3 Calculate the force pulling the trolley down the ramp.

....

....

Force = ... N
[2 marks]

Turn over for the next question

2 Two cyclists are cycling along a straight track. Cyclist 1 starts from rest at the track's start line. **Figure 2** shows the distance-time graph of Cyclist 1.

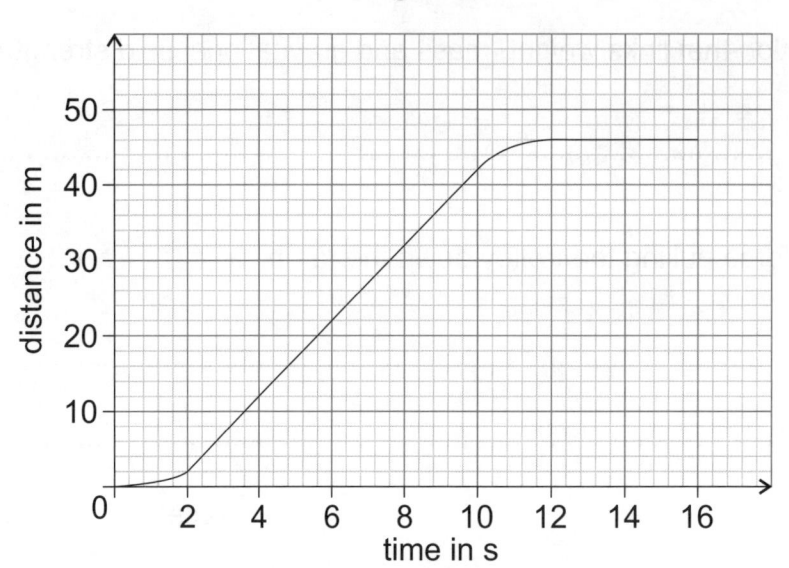

Figure 2

2.1 During which time period is Cyclist 1 decelerating?
Tick **one** box.

☐ From 0 s to 2 s ☐ From 10 s to 12 s

☐ From 4 s to 6 s ☐ From 12 s to 14 s

[1 mark]

2.2 Calculate the speed of Cyclist 1 between 2 and 10 seconds.

....

....

....

Speed = ... m/s
[3 marks]

Cyclist 2 crosses the start line at the same time as Cyclist 1.
Cyclist 2 travels at a constant speed of 4 m/s for 10 s and then stops suddenly.

2.3 Draw the distance-time graph of Cyclist 2 up to 16 s on **Figure 2**.
[2 marks]

2.4 Determine the time at which Cyclist 1 overtakes Cyclist 2.

....

Time = ... s
[1 mark]

3 Physical quantities can be either scalars or vectors.

3.1 Describe the difference between a scalar and a vector.

....

....
[1 mark]

Figure 3 shows a diagram of the forces acting on a car.

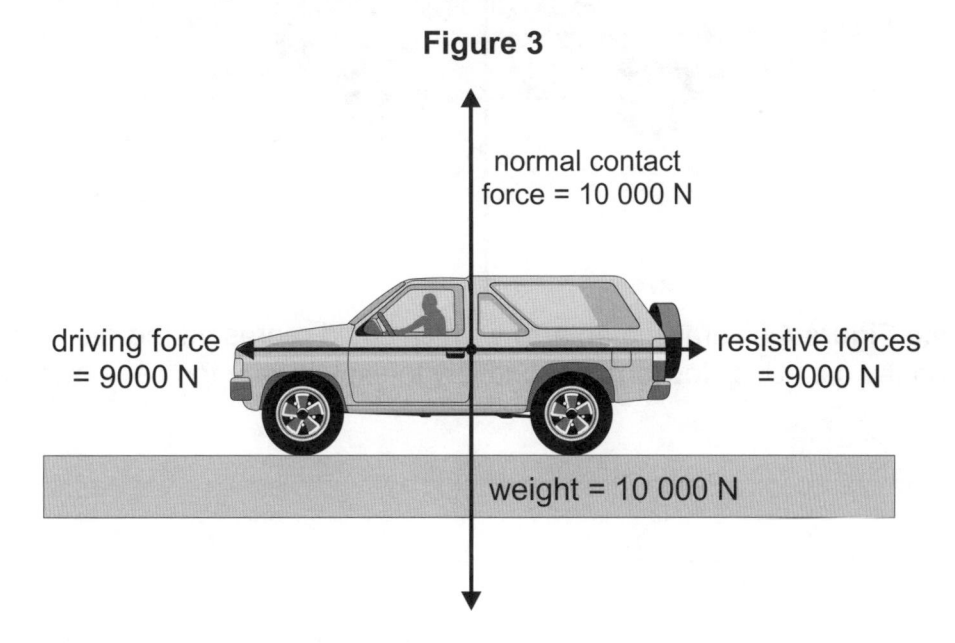

Figure 3

normal contact force = 10 000 N

driving force = 9000 N

resistive forces = 9000 N

weight = 10 000 N

3.2 Which of the following statements about the car in **Figure 3** is correct?
Tick **one** box.

☐ The car is accelerating.

☐ The car has an upwards resultant force acting on it.

☐ The forces on the car are in equilibrium.

☐ The car is slowing down.

[1 mark]

Question 3 continues on the next page

Turn over ▶

The car turns onto a dirt track. The driving force stays the same, but the car slows down. **Figure 4** shows an incomplete diagram of the forces acting on the car. The length of each arrow is proportional to the size of the force it represents.

Figure 4

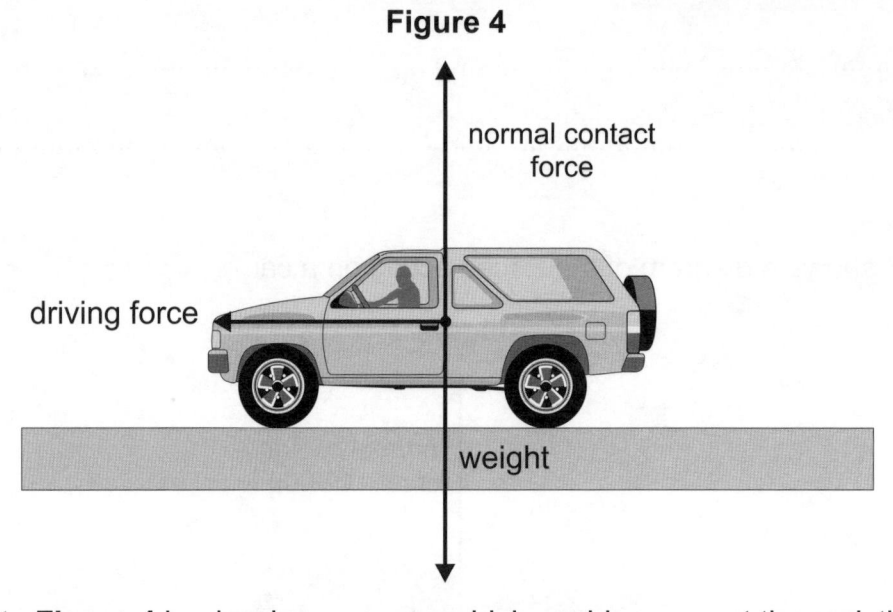

3.3 Complete **Figure 4** by drawing an arrow which could represent the resistive forces acting on the car. Use Newton's second law to explain why the car slows down.

....

....

....

....

....
[3 marks]

3.4 State the equation that links force, mass and acceleration.

....
[1 mark]

The car has a mass of 1800 kg.
The car brakes so that the net force acting on it is 1620 N.

3.5 Calculate the deceleration of the car.

....

....

Deceleration = ... m/s²
[2 marks]

The car stops. Person A and Person B get out of the car.
They pull a sled across a snowy field.
Person A exerts a force of 80 N north on the sled.
Person B exerts a force of 60 N east on the sled.

3.6 Draw a scale diagram of these two forces on the grid below.
Determine the magnitude and direction of the resultant of these two forces.
Give the direction as a clockwise angle from north.

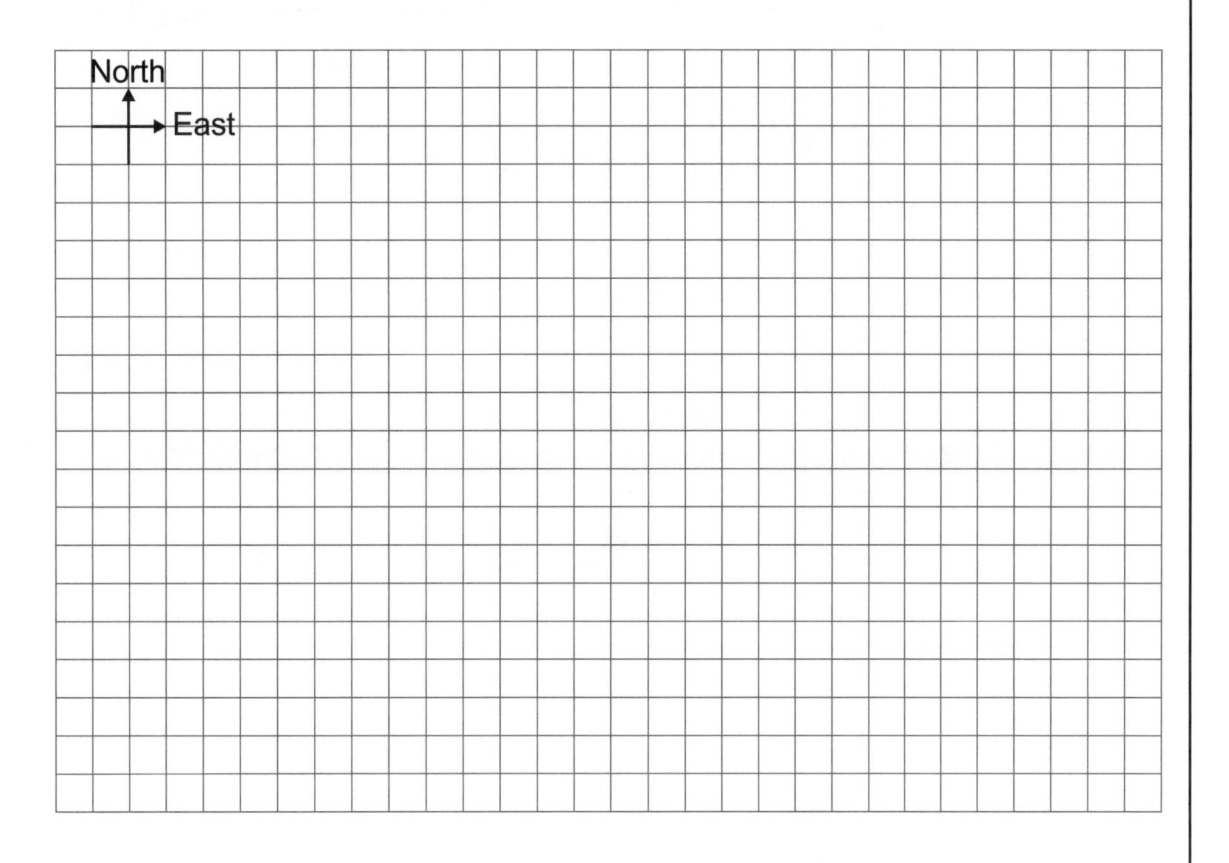

Magnitude of the resultant force = ... N

Direction = ... °

[3 marks]

Turn over for the next question

Leave blank

4 A student is investigating how the colour of an object affects its ability to absorb infrared radiation. He uses one flask that appears black, and one flask that appears white.

4.1 Explain why the black flask appears black, and the white flask appears white.

....

....

....

....

....

....

[3 marks]

The equipment the student uses in the experiment is shown in **Figure 5**.

Figure 5

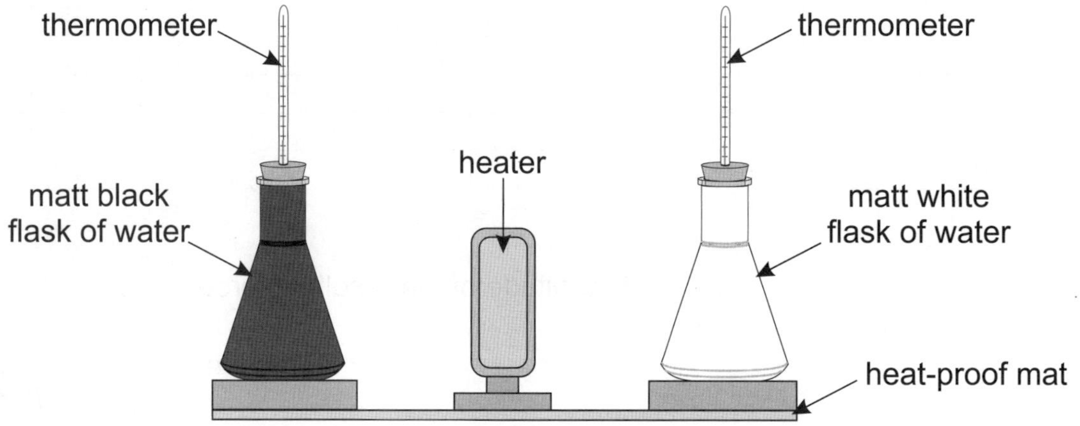

The student uses the following method:

1. Fill each flask with an equal amount of water at room temperature (20 °C).
2. Place each flask an equal distance from a heater.
3. Turn on the heater.
4. Record the temperature of the water in each flask every minute for 5 minutes.

4.2 State the independent variable in this experiment.

....

[1 mark]

4.3 State the dependent variable in this experiment.

....
[1 mark]

4.4 State **one** control variable in this experiment.

....
[1 mark]

The student repeats the experiment three times.
Table 1 shows the student's results for the black flask.

Table 1

Time in minutes	Temperature of black flask in °C		
	Trial 1	Trial 2	Trial 3
1	24	25	24
2	27	27	29
3	32	30	31
4	36	33	35
5	41	38	41

4.5 Using **Table 1**, calculate the mean temperature of the black flask after 5 minutes.

....

....

Mean temperature = ... °C
[2 marks]

Question 4 continues on the next page

Turn over ▶

4.6 Describe an experiment the student could do using the equipment in **Figure 5** to determine which flask is the better emitter of infrared radiation.

....
....
....
....
....
....
....
....

[4 marks]

5 A student uses a convex lens to produce an image of an object.

5.1 Which of the following correctly describes the image produced by a convex lens. Tick **one** box.

☐ The image produced by a convex lens is always real.

☐ The image produced by a convex lens is always virtual.

☐ The image produced by a convex lens can be real or virtual.

[1 mark]

Figure 6 shows an incomplete ray diagram of the convex lens being used to produce the image of the object. The principal focus on each side of the lens is labelled F.

Figure 6

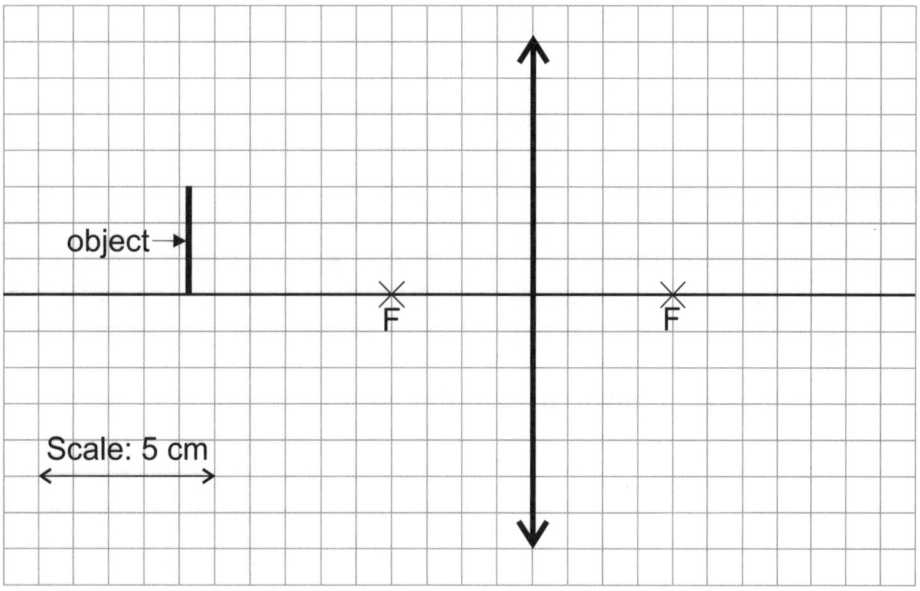

5.2 State the name given to the distance between the lens and the principal focus.

....

[1 mark]

5.3 Complete the ray diagram in **Figure 6** to show the image formed by the lens.

[3 marks]

5.4 Calculate the magnification of the lens when the object is at the distance shown in **Figure 6**. Use the correct equation from the Physics Equation Sheet.

....

....

Magnification = ...

[3 marks]

Turn over for the next question

Turn over ▶

6 Figure 7 shows the layers that make up the Earth's structure.

Figure 7

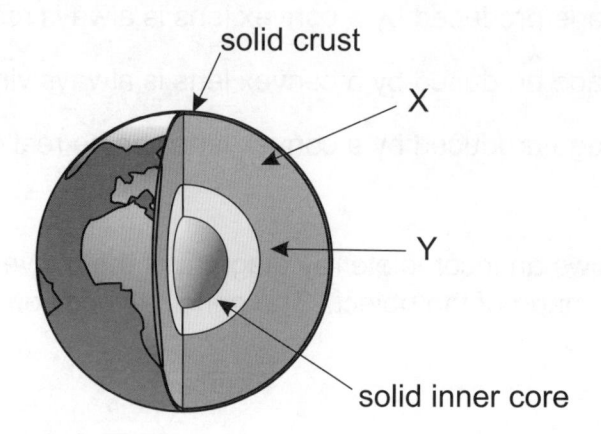

[Diagram of Earth's structure showing solid crust, X, Y, and solid inner core]

The core of the Earth is mostly made from magnetic materials.

6.1 Name **one** magnetic material.

....
[1 mark]

6.2 Explain why a compass points to the North Pole of the Earth.

....

....
[1 mark]

6.3 Give **one** reason why a compass might not be pointing to the North Pole of the Earth.

....
[1 mark]

Seismic waves are waves produced in the Earth by earthquakes.
P-waves and S-waves are two types of seismic waves.

6.4 Describe the difference between P-waves and S-waves.

....

....

....

....
[2 marks]

Figure 8 shows where S-waves can be detected on the surface of the Earth when an earthquake occurs at the point shown.

Figure 8

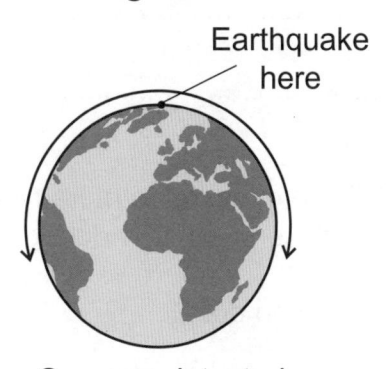

Earthquake here

S-waves detected where arrow shown

6.5 What conclusions can you draw from **Figure 8** about the composition of layers X and Y in **Figure 7**?

....

....

....

....

....
[2 marks]

Turn over for the next question   **Turn over ▶**

7 The International Space Station (ISS) and a communications satellite are each in a stable orbit around the Earth.
Table 2 shows the mass and orbital radius for each object.

Table 2

	Mass in kg	Orbital radius in km
ISS	420 000	6700
Communications Satellite	3500	42 000

7.1 Compare the orbital speeds of the ISS and the communications satellite. Justify your answer using information from **Table 2**.

....

....

....
[1 mark]

Astronauts that visit the ISS are exposed to more radiation than people on Earth. They experience a radiation dose of 80 mSv during a 6-month mission.

7.2 Explain what is meant by radiation dose.

....

....
[1 mark]

Cosmic rays and gamma rays are the main sources of the extra radiation that the astronauts are exposed to.

7.3 State **one** possible harmful effect of the human body being exposed to gamma rays.

....

....
[1 mark]

One source of cosmic rays are supernovae.

7.4 Describe what is meant by a supernova.
State the astronomical objects which can be left behind after a supernova.

....

....

....

....
[3 marks]

7.5 A supernova is one stage of a star's life cycle.
Describe the life cycle of a star that's the same size as the Sun, from its formation to the end of its life.

....

....

....

....

....

....

....

....

....

....
[6 marks]

Turn over for the next question

8 A student is investigating how a generator works.
The student connects a hand-powered generator to an oscilloscope as shown in **Figure 9**.

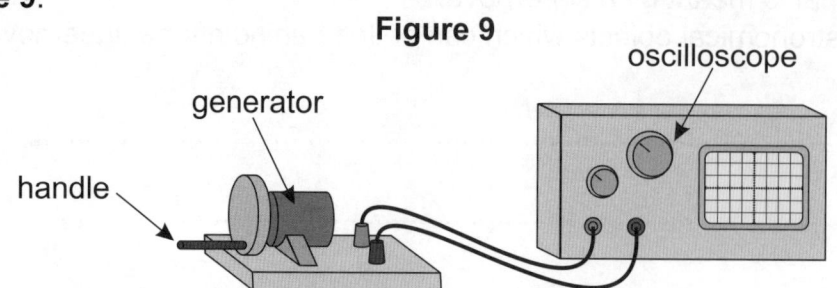

Figure 9

The student turns the handle of the generator at a constant rate.
The oscilloscope is used to monitor how the potential difference across the generator varies with time.
Figure 10 shows the trace produced by the oscilloscope.

Figure 10

8.1 State the name given to the type of generator the student is using.
Use **Figure 10** to justify your answer.

....

....
[2 marks]

8.2 Using **Figure 10**, determine the number of times the handle was turned each second.

....

....

....

Number of rotations per second = ...
[2 marks]

The student uses another generator connected to a radio transmitter to produce radio waves with a frequency of 39.2 kHz. Radio waves travel through air at 3.00 × 10⁸ m/s.

8.3 Calculate the wavelength of radio waves produced.

....

....

Wavelength = ... m
[2 marks]

The radio waves reach a receiver where they induce oscillations in an electrical circuit. The electrical signals are converted into sound waves by the loudspeaker shown in **Figure 11**.

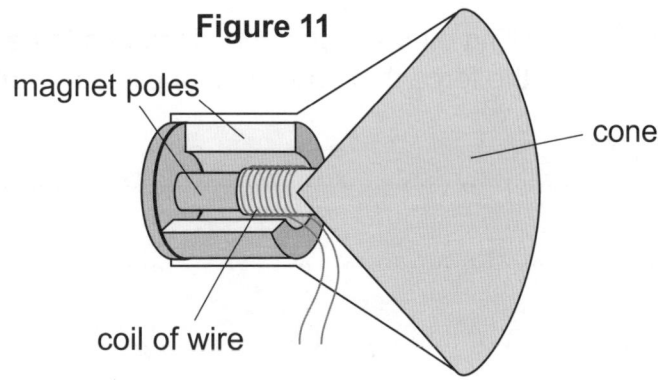

Figure 11

The current in the loudspeaker's coil is within the magnetic field of the magnet. This causes a force on the coil which causes the cone to move. The vibrations of the cone cause sound waves to be produced.

When 10.4 m of the coil was inside and at 90° to the magnetic field, the force on the coil was 0.880 N. The magnetic flux density of the magnet is 0.160 T.

8.4 Calculate the current through the coil at this point.
Use the correct equation from the Physics Equation Sheet.
Give your answer to 3 significant figures.

....

....

....

....

Current = ... A
[3 marks]

Turn over for the next question

9 Some children are playing in a playground. They use a plank and a rock to create a catapult. A child pushes down on the end of the catapult as shown in **Figure 12**.

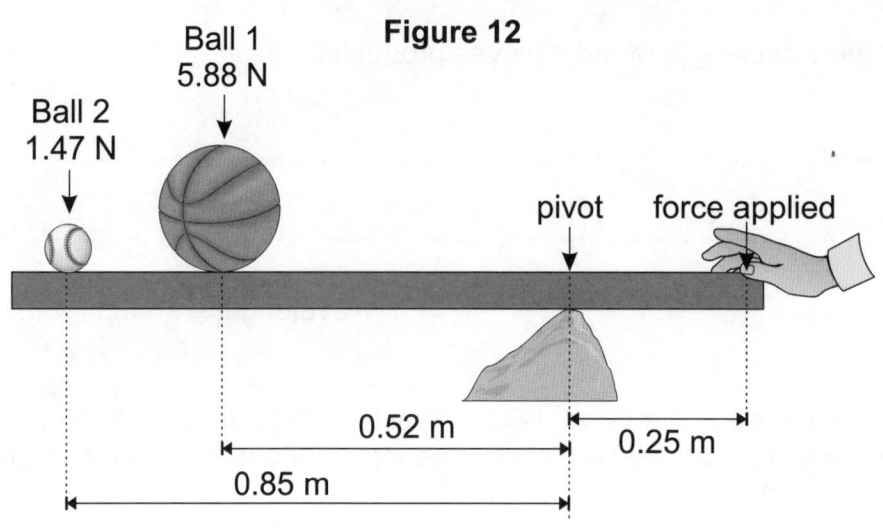

Figure 12

Ball 1: 5.88 N
Ball 2: 1.47 N
pivot
force applied
0.52 m
0.25 m
0.85 m

9.1 To stop the balls from rolling off the plank, the plank has to be balanced perfectly horizontally. Calculate the force that should be applied in **Figure 12**.

Force = ... N
[5 marks]

The child pushes down quickly on the end of the catapult, but the balls do not travel very fast into the air.

9.2 Suggest and explain how the students could adapt their catapult to launch the balls faster into the air.

[2 marks]

Another child, Child D, is hanging from a climbing frame, as shown in **Figure 13**.

Figure 13

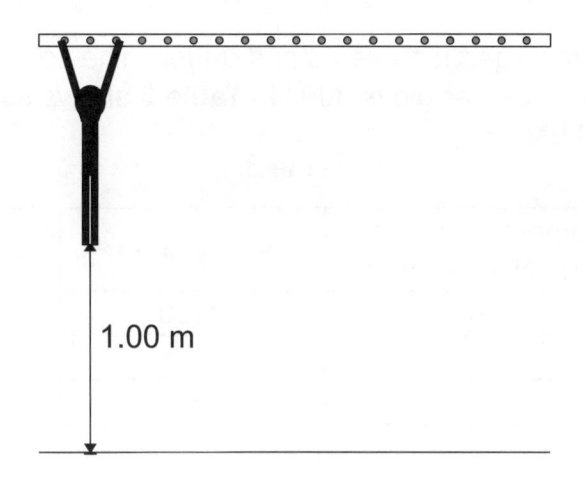

1.00 m

Child D lets go of the climbing frame, and falls to the ground.
They land on their feet. The acceleration due to gravity is 9.8 m/s².

9.3 Calculate the speed at which Child D hits the ground.

Speed = ... m/s
[3 marks]

9.4 Child D has a mass of 30.0 kg.
They experience a force of 266 N when they land on the ground.
Calculate the time it takes for them to come to a stop.

Time = ... s
[2 marks]

Question 9 continues on the next page

Turn over ▶

The council are planning to expand the playground.
They want to use a material on the ground which will help improve
the safety of the playground and prevent injury.

The park is for children aged nine years and under. The council find that the average weight of a nine-year-old is 300 N. **Table 3** shows some properties of the materials they could use.

Table 3

	Compression under 300 N force (mm)	Density (kg/m³)	Deforms elastically?
Material A	0	2400	No
Material B	2.5	400	Yes
Material C	1.5	650	No

9.5 Evaluate which material the council should use to cover the ground, in order to make the playground safer. Use ideas about momentum in your answer.

[6 marks]

10 A student is investigating the magnetic field produced by a current-carrying wire. They twist the current-carrying wire into a solenoid.

10.1 Explain why twisting a current-carrying wire into a solenoid will increase the strength of the magnetic field produced around the wire.

....

....

....

....

....

....
[3 marks]

The student investigates how the strength of the magnetic field inside a solenoid changes with the number of turns on the solenoid per unit length.

They keep the current through the coil constant, but change the number of turns in each centimetre of the solenoid.

Table 4 shows the student's results.

Table 4

Turns per centimetre	Magnetic flux density (T)
1	5.0×10^{-5}
2	1.1×10^{-4}
3	1.5×10^{-4}
4	1.8×10^{-4}
5	2.6×10^{-4}
6	2.9×10^{-4}
7	3.5×10^{-4}
8	4.0×10^{-4}

Question 10 continues on the next page

Turn over ▶

10.2 **Figure 14** shows an incomplete graph of the student's results.
Complete **Figure 14** by plotting the remaining points and drawing a line of best fit.

Figure 14

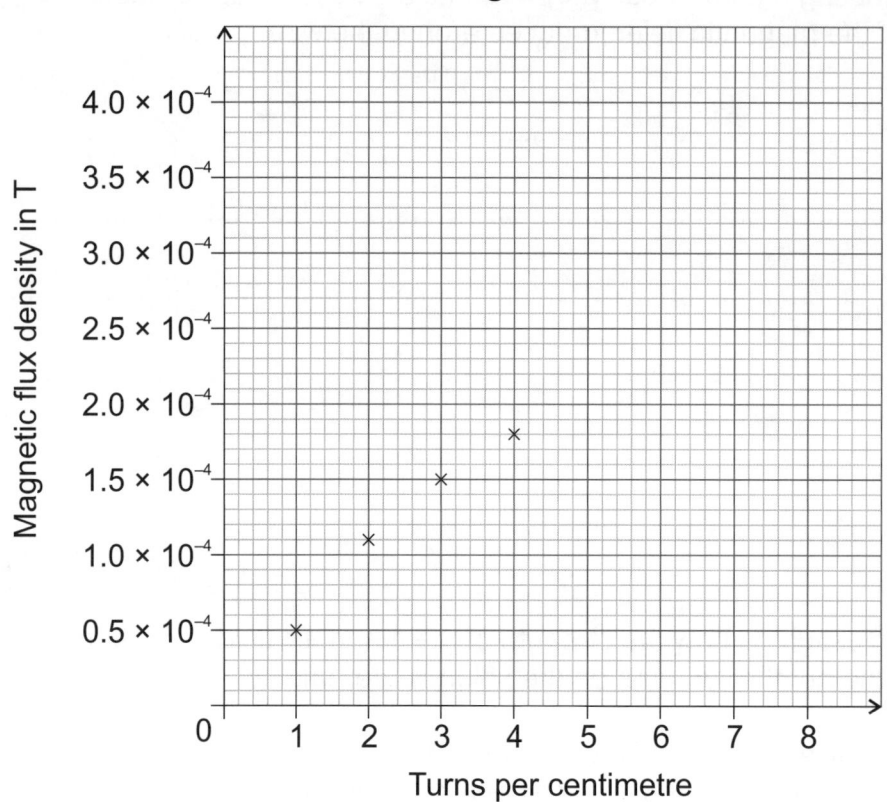

[Graph: Magnetic flux density in T (y-axis, 0 to 4.0 × 10⁻⁴) vs Turns per centimetre (x-axis, 0 to 8). Plotted points at approximately (1, 0.5 × 10⁻⁴), (2, 1.1 × 10⁻⁴), (3, 1.5 × 10⁻⁴), (4, 1.8 × 10⁻⁴).]

[2 marks]

10.3 Draw a conclusion for the experiment, using **Figure 14**.

....

....

[1 mark]

Magnetic flux density is a measure of the strength of a magnetic field.

The relationship between the magnetic flux density and the number of turns per unit length is described by the equation:

magnetic flux density = μ × turns per centimetre × current

where μ is a constant.

10.4 The current through the solenoid was 0.4 A.
Using **Figure 14**, determine the value of μ.

....

....

....

....

....

....

....

μ = ...
[3 marks]

END OF QUESTIONS

GCSE Physics Equation Sheet

$p = h\rho g$	p pressure due to a column of liquid h height of column ρ density of liquid g gravitational field strength
$v^2 - u^2 = 2as$	v final velocity u initial velocity a acceleration s distance
$F = \dfrac{m\Delta v}{\Delta t}$	F force $m\Delta v$ change in momentum Δt time taken
$E_e = \frac{1}{2}ke^2$	E_e elastic potential energy k spring constant e extension
$\Delta E = mc\Delta\theta$	ΔE change in thermal energy m mass c specific heat capacity $\Delta\theta$ change in temperature
period = $\dfrac{1}{\text{frequency}}$	
magnification = $\dfrac{\text{image height}}{\text{object height}}$	
$F = BIl$	F force on a current-carrying conductor (at right angles to the field) B magnetic flux density I current l length
$E = mL$	E thermal energy for a change of state m mass L specific latent heat
$\dfrac{V_p}{V_s} = \dfrac{n_p}{n_s}$	V_p potential difference across primary coil V_s potential difference across secondary coil n_p number of turns in primary coil n_s number of turns in secondary coil
$V_s I_s = V_p I_p$	V_s potential difference across secondary coil I_s current in secondary coil V_p potential difference across primary coil I_p current in primary coil
For gases: pV = constant	p pressure V volume

GCSE Physics

Set B Paper 1

Higher Tier

In addition to this paper you should have:
- A ruler.
- A calculator.

Centre name
Centre number
Candidate number

Surname
Other names
Candidate signature

Time allowed:
- 1 hour 45 minutes

Instructions to candidates
- Write your name and other details in the spaces provided above.
- Answer **all** questions in the spaces provided.
- Do all rough work on the paper.
- Cross out any work you do not want to be marked.

Information for candidates
- The marks available are given in brackets at the end of each question.
- There are 100 marks available for this paper.
- You are allowed to use a calculator.
- You should use good English and present your answers in a clear and organised way.
- For Questions 6.2 and 8.3 ensure that your answers have a clear and logical structure, include the right scientific terms, spelt correctly, and include detailed, relevant information.

Advice to candidates
- In calculations show clearly how you worked out your answers.
- An equation sheet is included at the back of this paper.

Answer **all** questions in the spaces provided

1 An electrician connects a kettle to the mains electricity supply using an electric cable.
The cable has three wires: a live wire, a neutral wire and an earth wire.
Each wire is surrounded by insulation of a different colour.

1.1 State the approximate potential difference of the UK mains supply.

....
[1 mark]

The electrician switches the kettle on.
He measures the current in the earth wire and finds the kettle is working normally.

1.2 State the current in the earth wire and explain your answer.

....

....
[2 marks]

1.3 Write down the formula which links power, current and potential difference.

....
[1 mark]

1.4 The kettle has a power of 1.61 kW. Calculate the current in the live wire.

....

....

Current = ... A
[2 marks]

1.5 The kettle contains a circuit called a thermostat. The thermostat detects when the water has reached 100 °C and switches the kettle off. The circuit contains a component that decreases in resistance as its temperature increases.
Name this component.

....
[1 mark]

2 **Figure 1** shows an archer preparing to fire an arrow.

Figure 1

2.1 When she pulls back the string of the bow, there is an energy transfer.
20 J of energy transfers from the chemical store in her muscles.
Name the energy store of the bow that the energy is transferred to.

....
[1 mark]

2.2 Energy can be stored.
What other words can be used to describe something that can happen to energy?
Tick **two** boxes.

☐ dissipated

☐ wasted

☐ destroyed

☐ created

[1 mark]

2.3 The archer releases the arrow.
15 J of energy is transferred into the arrow's kinetic energy store.
Suggest where the rest of the energy is transferred to.

....
[1 mark]

Question 2 continues on the next page

Turn over ▶

2.4 Write down the equation that links efficiency, useful output energy transfer and total input energy transfer.

....
[1 mark]

2.5 Calculate the efficiency of the bow.

....

....

Efficiency = ... %
[2 marks]

Leave blank

3 A tennis player is testing a tennis ball by hitting it with a tennis racket. As the player hits the ball, energy is transferred to the ball's kinetic energy store.

The mass of the tennis ball is 58 g.
The speed of the ball immediately after leaving the racket is 25 m/s.

3.1 Write down the formula that links kinetic energy, mass and speed.

....

[1 mark]

3.2 Calculate how much energy the ball has in its kinetic energy store as it leaves the racket.
Give your answer to two significant figures.

....

....

....

Energy = ... J

[3 marks]

3.3 The player hits the tennis ball again, and it follows the path shown in **Figure 2**.

Figure 2

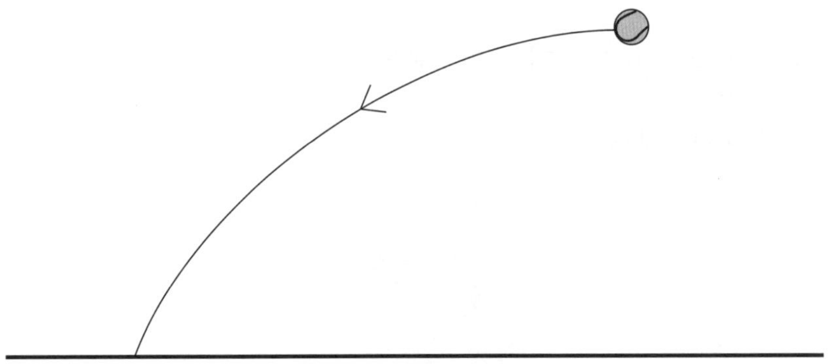

The ball hits the ground at a faster speed than it left the racket.
Explain why. Use ideas about energy in your answer.

....

....

....

[2 marks]

Turn over for the next question

Turn over ▶

4 **Table 1** shows the typical densities of a number of substances.

Leave blank

Table 1

Material	State	Density in g/cm^3
Sandstone	Solid	2.2
Granite	Solid	2.6
Limestone	Solid	2.8
Water	Liquid	1.0
Ethanol	Liquid	0.8
Olive oil	Liquid	0.9

4.1 Describe the pattern seen in **Table 1**.

....

....
[1 mark]

4.2 Explain the pattern seen in **Table 1** using the particle model.

....

....

....
[2 marks]

Figure 3 shows a volcanic rock called pumice.
Pumice has a density of 0.5 g/cm^3.
Air has a density of 0.001 g/cm^3.

Figure 3

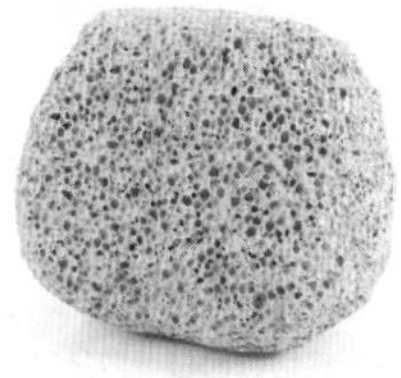

4.3 Explain why pumice does not fit the pattern described in question part **4.1**.

....

....

....
[2 marks]

A student wants to measure the density of a rock.
She puts 500 cm³ of water into a beaker.
She then puts the rock into the water as shown in **Figure 4**.

Figure 4

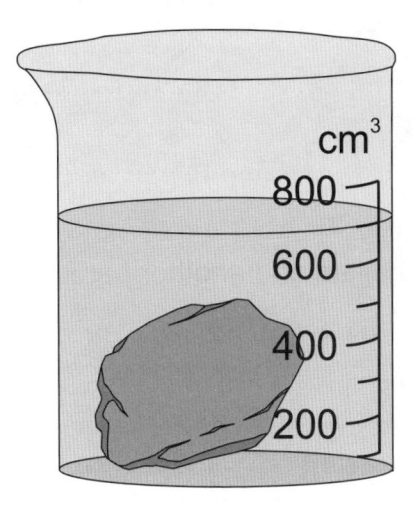

4.4 Calculate the volume of the rock shown in **Figure 4**.

....

....

Volume = ... cm³
[1 mark]

4.5 Suggest how the student could improve the precision of the volume measurement.

....

....
[1 mark]

The mass of the rock is 420 g.

4.6 Suggest the material that the rock is made from.
Justify your answer with a calculation and data from **Table 1**.

....

....

....

....
[3 marks]

Turn over for the next question

Turn over ▶

5 Scientists are trying to develop a nuclear reactor that can use nuclear fusion reactions to provide power.
One such nuclear fusion reaction involves two isotopes of hydrogen, ^2_1H and ^3_1H.

5.1 Explain how you can tell that ^2_1H and ^3_1H are isotopes of the same element.

....

....
[1 mark]

5.2 The fusion reaction forms helium and another particle:

$$^2_1H + {}^3_1H \rightarrow {}^4_2He + {}^A_BX$$

Calculate the values A and B.

....

....

....

A = ... , B = ...
[2 marks]

5.3 What particle does X represent in this fusion reaction?
Tick **one** box.

☐ Electron

☐ Proton

☐ Neutron

[1 mark]

5.4 Fusion reactions are difficult to achieve. This is because large forces are needed to get the nuclei close enough for fusion to occur.
Explain why large forces are required for fusion to occur.

....

....

....
[3 marks]

6 A student is investigating two different types of home insulation, A and B. For each type of insulation, he sets up the apparatus as shown in **Figure 5**.

Figure 5

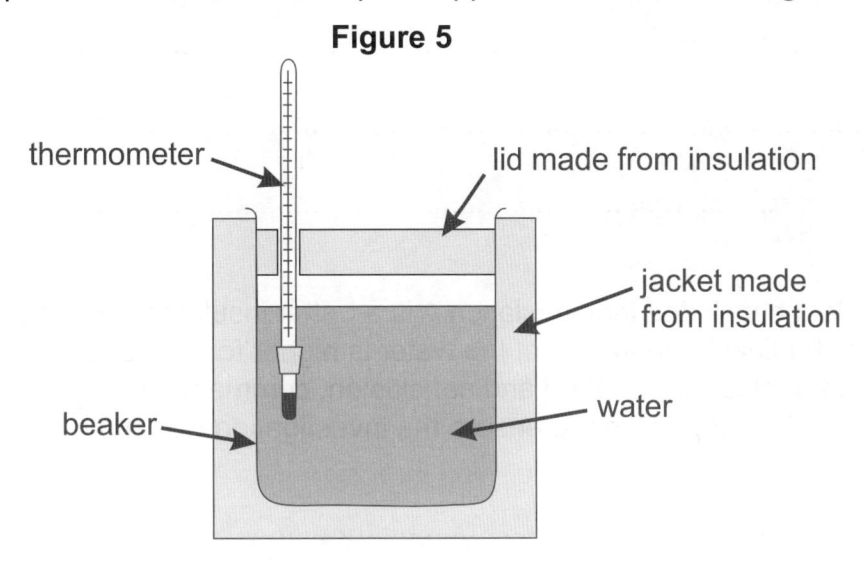

The student uses the following method:

- Surround the beaker with a 15 mm thickness of insulation A.
- Measure the temperature of the room and make sure it is 21 °C.
- Pour 200 cm³ of hot water into the beaker.
- Place a 15 mm thick lid of insulation A with a small hole in it on top.
- Put a thermometer through the hole and record the temperature of the water every minute.
- Repeat the steps above with the same equipment using insulation B instead of insulation A.

Figure 6 shows a graph of his results.

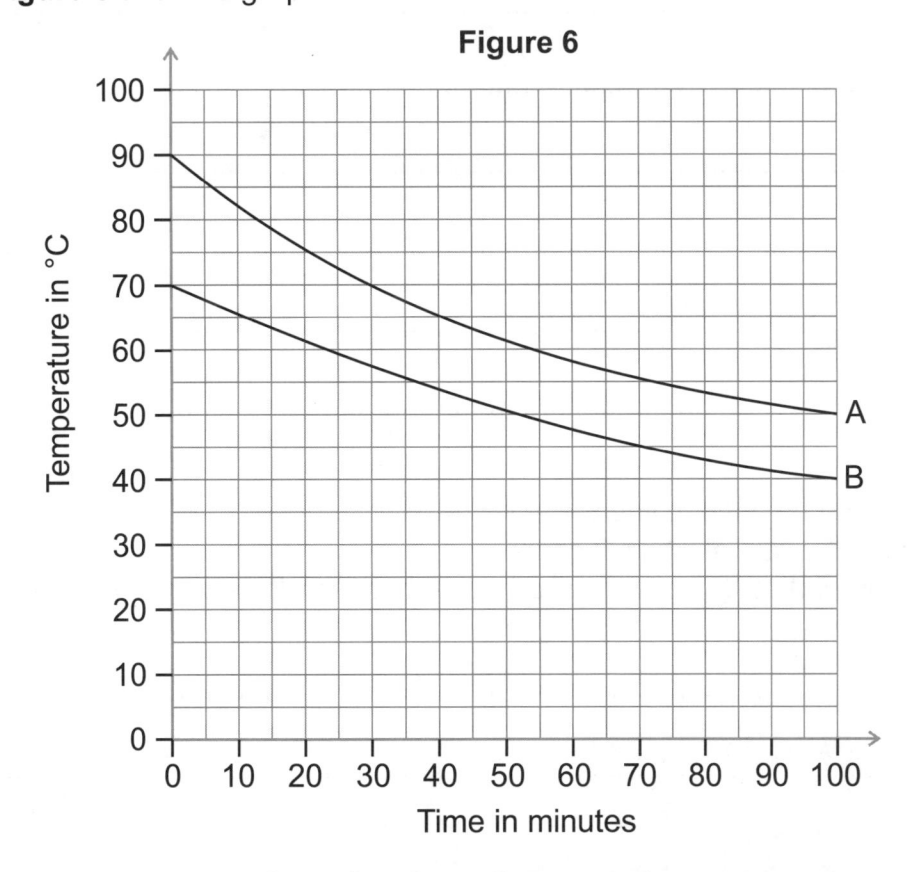

Figure 6

Question 6 continues on the next page

6.1 Explain why the hot water cools down.

....

....

....
[2 marks]

6.2 The student concludes that insulation A is a better insulator than insulation B because the final temperature of the water is higher for insulation A.
Evaluate the student's method and conclusion, commenting on validity and the steps taken to ensure the investigation was a fair test.

....

....

....

....

....

....

....

....

....

....

....
[6 marks]

6.3 Home insulation can be used to line the walls of a house to reduce the rate at which it cools.
Give **two** other properties of the walls of a house that can affect its rate of cooling.

1. ....

2. ....
[2 marks]

7 A student is designing and building a sensor which measures the thickness of tissue paper. He decides to use a light dependent resistor (LDR) in the sensor.

7.1 Draw the circuit symbol for an LDR.

[1 mark]

The student first investigates how the resistance of the LDR he is using varies with light intensity. **Table 2** shows his results.

Table 2

Intensity in W/m²	Resistance in kΩ
0	1000
2	500
4	340
6	270
8	240
10	220
12	200

Figure 7 shows an incomplete graph of his results.

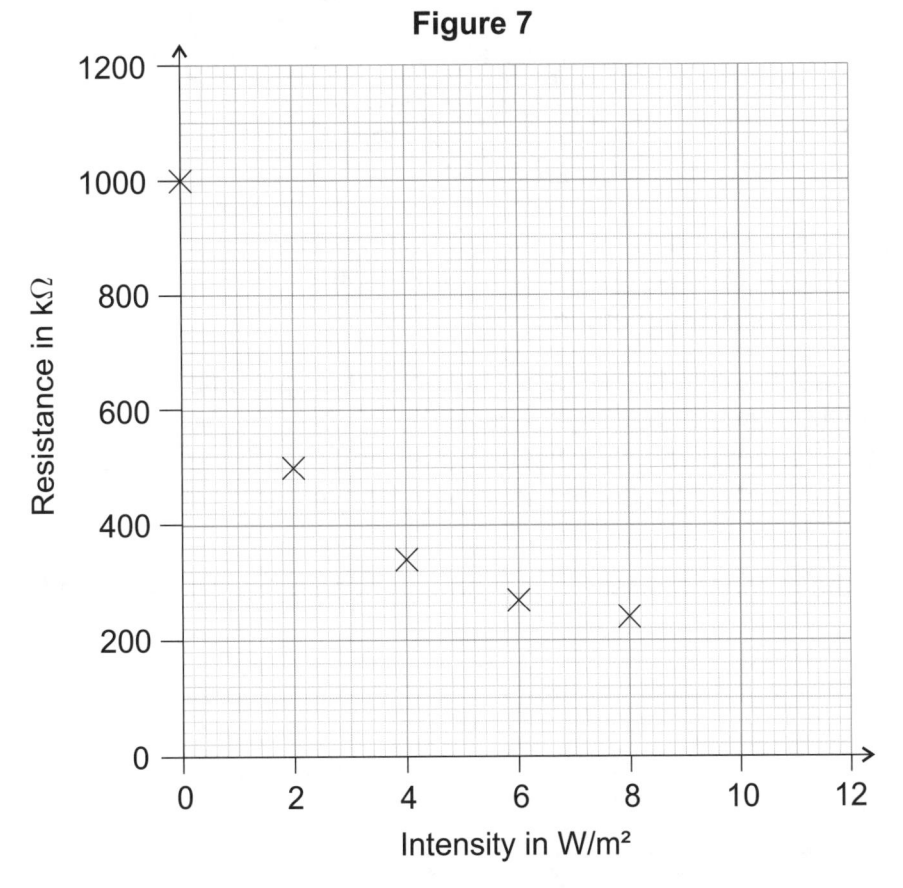

Figure 7

Question 7 continues on the next page

7.2 Complete the graph in **Figure 7** using the data from **Table 2**.
Draw a line of best fit for the data.

[2 marks]

Leave blank

7.3 State the independent variable in this experiment.

....

[1 mark]

7.4 Use the graph to describe the relationship between light intensity and the resistance of an LDR.

....

....

[2 marks]

The student uses the apparatus shown in **Figure 8** to make his sensor.

Figure 8

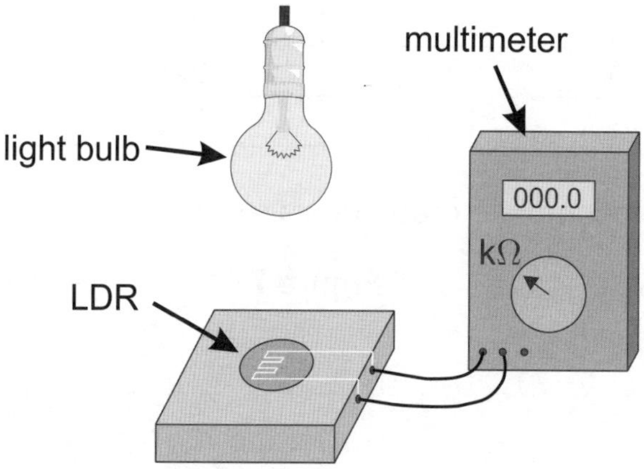

To calibrate his sensor, he turns on the light bulb and uses the multimeter to measure the resistance of the LDR.
He then uses the following method:

1. Put one sheet of white tissue paper between the light bulb and the LDR. Record the resistance of the LDR.
2. Add another sheet of identical tissue paper and record the resistance of the LDR.
3. Repeat step 2 until 8 sheets of tissue paper have been added in total.

7.5 Explain how the number of tissue paper sheets affects the resistance of the LDR.

....

....

....

[1 mark]

7.6 Suggest **one** way the student can make his measurements as accurate as possible.

Leave blank

....

....

[1 mark]

Each sheet of white tissue paper is 0.05 mm thick.
The student plots a graph of tissue paper thickness against LDR resistance, shown in **Figure 9**.

Figure 9

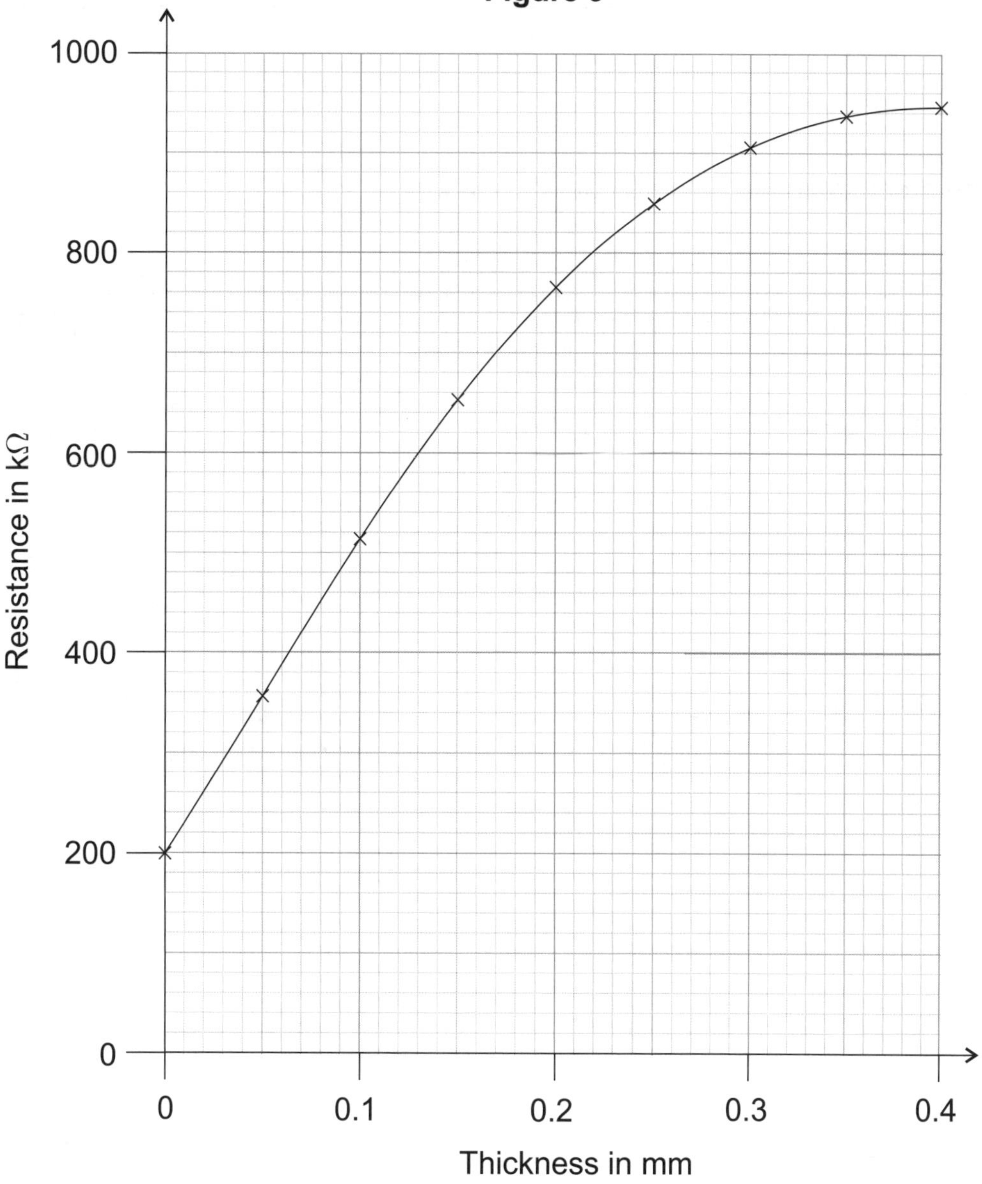

Question 7 continues on the next page

Turn over ▶

7.7 The student places a new piece of tissue paper with an unknown thickness over the sensor.
The resistance of the LDR is 600 kΩ.
Use the graph in **Figure 9** to estimate the thickness of the tissue paper.

Thickness = ... mm
[1 mark]

7.8 Explain why the student's sensor would be less accurate for tissue paper thicknesses above 0.4 mm.

....

....
[2 marks]

7.9 Suggest **one** other limitation of the student's sensor.

....
[1 mark]

8 A teacher is demonstrating a fire piston. The fire piston contains air and some char cloth at the bottom, as shown in **Figure 10**. Char cloth is a flammable fabric that ignites when it reaches a certain temperature. When the teacher pushes the plunger down quickly, the char cloth catches fire.

Figure 10

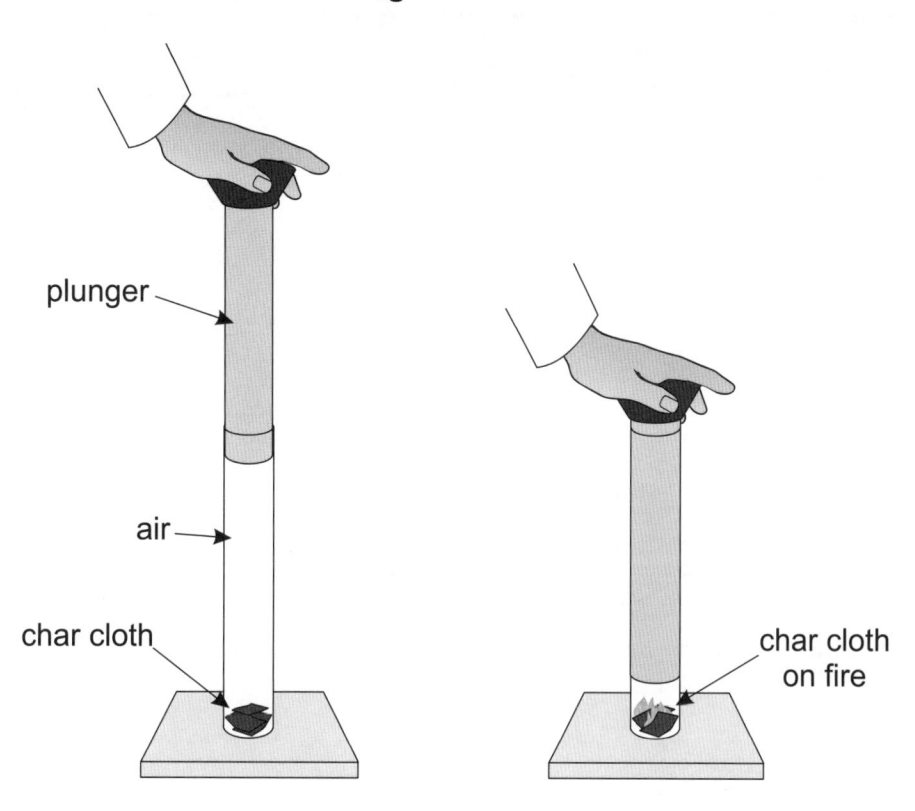

8.1 Explain why the char cloth ignites.

....

....

....
[2 marks]

8.2 The teacher keeps the plunger pressed in and the char cloth continues to burn.
The temperature of the air continues to increase.
Describe how the motion of the air particles changes as the temperature increases.

....
[1 mark]

Question 8 continues on the next page

Turn over ▶

8.3 Explain why the temperature and pressure of the air inside the piston change when the char cloth is burning. Use ideas about particles in your answer.

....
....
....
....
....
....
....
....
....

[6 marks]

9 A student is investigating the total resistance in electric circuits. She sets up the circuit shown in **Figure 11**.

Figure 11

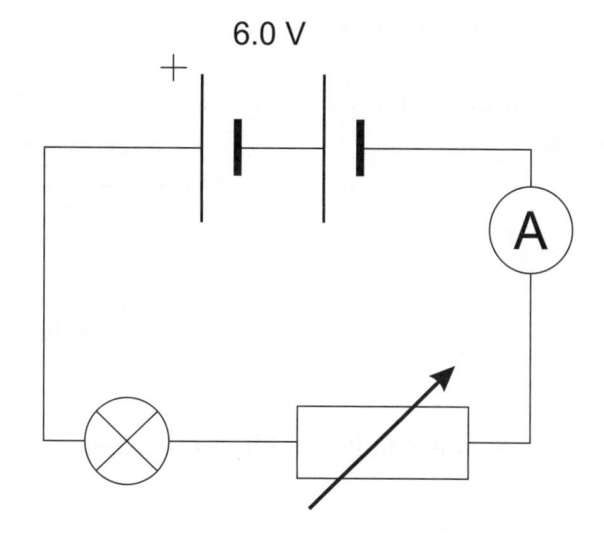

9.1 The student sets the variable resistor to 10 Ω and the ammeter measures a current of 40 mA. Calculate the total resistance in the circuit.

....

....

Total resistance = ... Ω
[3 marks]

9.2 Calculate the resistance of the filament lamp.

....

....

Resistance = ... Ω
[1 mark]

Question 9 continues on the next page

Turn over ▶

9.3 The student now sets the variable resistor to 100 Ω and the ammeter measures a current of 30 mA.
Calculate the resistance of the filament lamp now.

....

....

....

....

Resistance = ... Ω
[2 marks]

9.4 Explain why the resistance of the filament lamp changes.

....

....

....

....

[3 marks]

10 **Figure 12** shows a graph of how the temperature of some water varies with time. The water is heated in a large beaker using a heater of constant power.

Figure 12

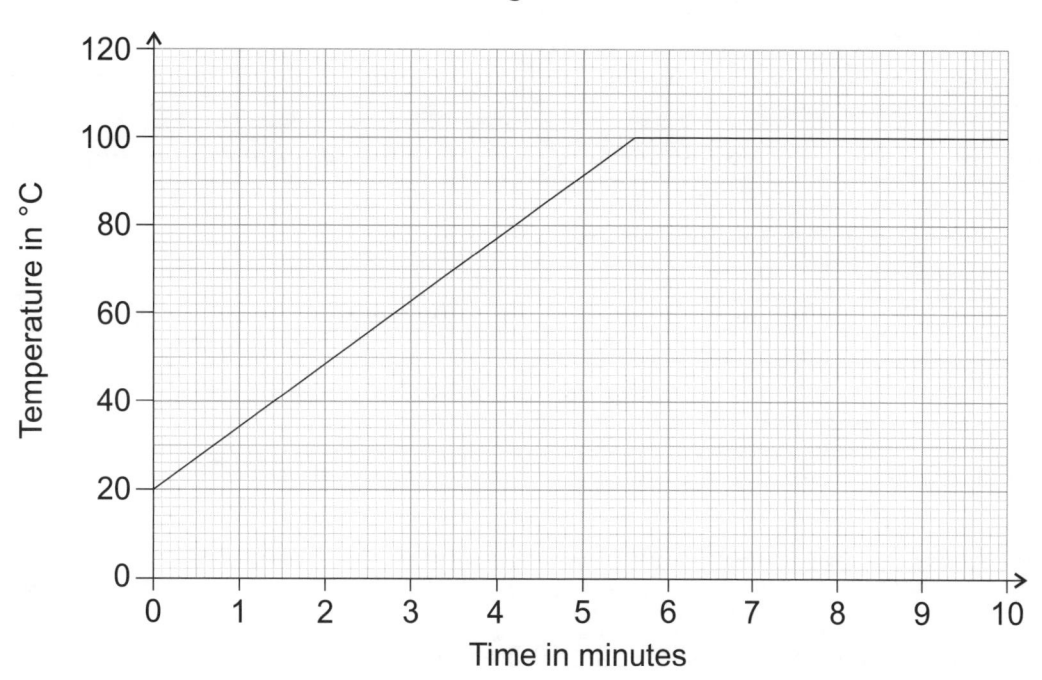

The mass of the water at the beginning of the experiment was 2.0 kg.
After 10 minutes, the mass of water was 1.8 kg.

10.1 Calculate the energy transferred to the water when the temperature increases from 20 °C to 100 °C.
The specific heat capacity of water = 4200 J/kg°C.
Use the correct equation from the Physics Equation Sheet.

....

....

Energy transferred = ... J
[2 marks]

10.2 Calculate the power of the heater.

....

....

....

Power = ... W
[3 marks]

Question 10 continues on the next page

10.3 Calculate the specific latent heat of vaporisation of water.
Use the correct equation from the Physics Equation Sheet.

....

....

....

....

....

....

....

[5 marks]

10.4 The value calculated in question part **10.3** for the specific latent heat of vaporisation is higher than the actual value. Suggest **one** reason why.

....

....

....

[2 marks]

11 Scientists are developing a battery that is powered by radioactive waste.
The radioactive waste is produced by a nuclear power station which uses nuclear fission. Carbon-12 is used to help the reaction.
The nuclear reactor gradually turns the carbon-12 into radioactive carbon-14.

11.1 Carbon has an atomic number of 6.
Describe how the carbon nucleus will change in the reactor.
Suggest how this change occurs.

....

....

....
[3 marks]

Carbon-14 decays to form nitrogen. **Figure 13** shows how the amount of carbon-14 nuclei in a sample changes over time.

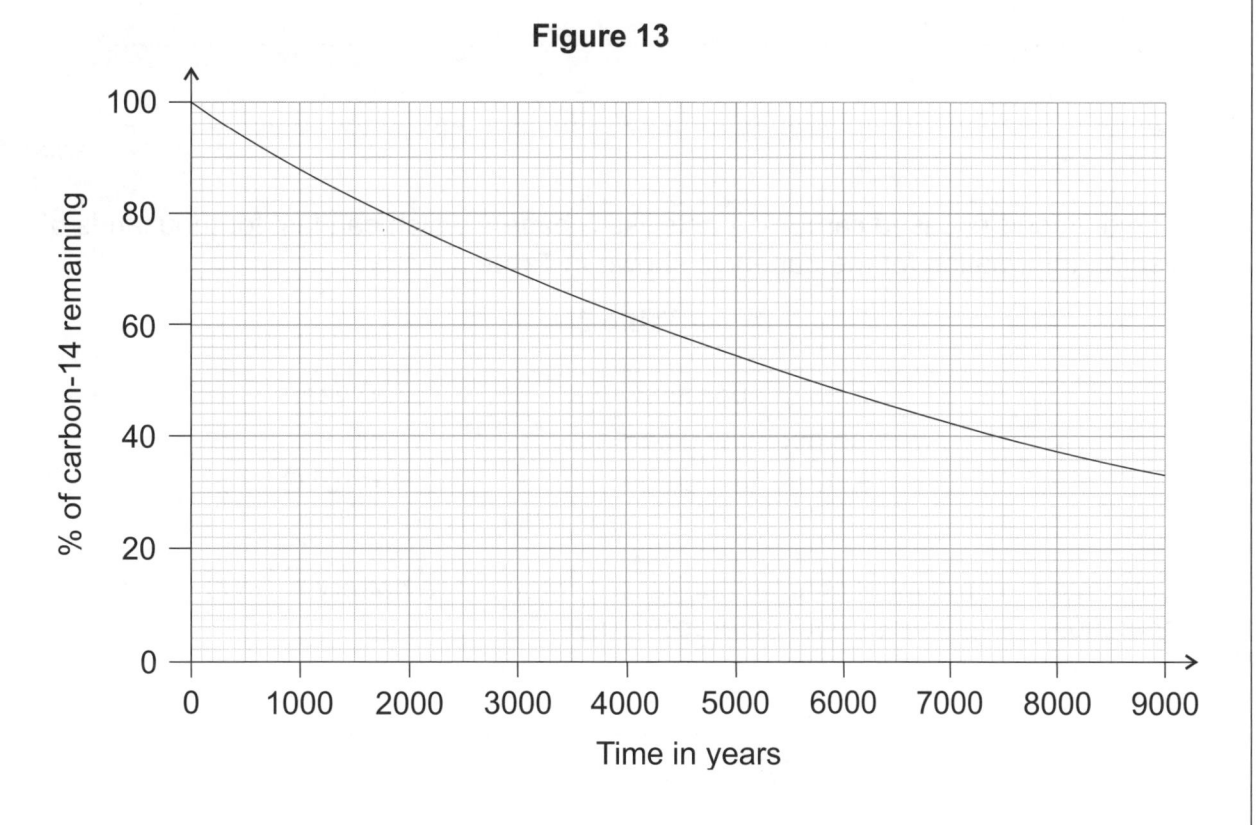

Figure 13

Question 11 continues on the next page

11.2 Use **Figure 13** to calculate the activity of carbon-12 after 11 400 years as a fraction of the original activity.

....

....

....

Fraction = ...
[2 marks]

11.3 Radioactive substances can cause harm to humans. The scientists extract some carbon-14 from the nuclear reactor and encase it in diamond.
Suggest how the diamond casing helps to prevent contamination and irradiation.

....

....

....

[2 marks]

The diamond-encased carbon-14 acts like a battery which can last for thousands of years. Information for the battery is shown in **Table 3**.

Table 3

Time of operation	5700 years
Average potential difference	2.0 V
Energy delivered	2.7×10^3 GJ

11.4 Calculate the amount of charge that passes through the battery in 5700 years of operation. Give your answer in teracoulombs, TC.

....

....

Charge = ... TC
[2 marks]

11.5 Diamond is very resistant to scratches and erosion over long periods of time. Explain why this is important for these batteries.

....

....
[1 mark]

11.6 Suggest **one** advantage and **one** disadvantage of using this battery.

Advantage: ....

....

Disadvantage: ....

....
[2 marks]

END OF QUESTIONS

GCSE Physics Equation Sheet

$p = h\rho g$	p pressure due to a column of liquid h height of column ρ density of liquid g gravitational field strength
$v^2 - u^2 = 2as$	v final velocity u initial velocity a acceleration s distance
$F = \dfrac{m\Delta v}{\Delta t}$	F force $m\Delta v$ change in momentum Δt time taken
$E_e = \tfrac{1}{2}ke^2$	E_e elastic potential energy k spring constant e extension
$\Delta E = mc\Delta\theta$	ΔE change in thermal energy m mass c specific heat capacity $\Delta\theta$ change in temperature
period = $\dfrac{1}{\text{frequency}}$	
magnification = $\dfrac{\text{image height}}{\text{object height}}$	
$F = BIl$	F force on a current-carrying conductor (at right angles to the field) B magnetic flux density I current l length
$E = mL$	E thermal energy for a change of state m mass L specific latent heat
$\dfrac{V_p}{V_s} = \dfrac{n_p}{n_s}$	V_p potential difference across primary coil V_s potential difference across secondary coil n_p number of turns in primary coil n_s number of turns in secondary coil
$V_s I_s = V_p I_p$	V_s potential difference across secondary coil I_s current in secondary coil V_p potential difference across primary coil I_p current in primary coil
For gases: pV = constant	p pressure V volume

GCSE Physics

Set B Paper 2

Higher Tier

In addition to this paper you should have:
- A ruler.
- A calculator.
- A protractor

Centre name				
Centre number				
Candidate number				

Time allowed:
- 1 hour 45 minutes

Surname	
Other names	
Candidate signature	

Instructions to candidates
- Write your name and other details in the spaces provided above.
- Answer **all** questions in the spaces provided.
- Do all rough work on the paper.
- Cross out any work you do not want to be marked.

Information for candidates
- The marks available are given in brackets at the end of each question.
- There are 100 marks available for this paper.
- You are allowed to use a calculator.
- You should use good English and present your answers in a clear and organised way.
- For Questions 3.1 and 6.3 ensure that your answers have a clear and logical structure, include the right scientific terms, spelt correctly, and include detailed, relevant information.

For examiner's use

Q	Attempt Nº 1	2	3	Q	Attempt Nº 1	2	3
1				6			
2				7			
3				8			
4				9			
5				10			
				Total			

Advice to candidates
- In calculations show clearly how you worked out your answers.
- An equation sheet is included at the back of this paper.

Answer **all** questions in the spaces provided

1 Eta Carinae A is a star in the Milky Way galaxy.
It is surrounded by a cloud of gas and dust.

1.1 The mass of Eta Carinae A is approximately 1.8×10^{32} kg.
The mass of the Sun is 2.0×10^{30} kg.
Calculate the ratio of the mass of Eta Carinae A to the mass of the Sun.

....

Ratio = ...
[1 mark]

1.2 The measurement for the mass of Eta Carinae A is not very accurate.
Suggest **two** reasons why it is a difficult to get an accurate measurement of the mass of Eta Carinae A.

1. ....

2. ....
[2 marks]

Elements are being formed in the core of Eta Carinae A.

1.3 Name and describe the process by which elements are formed inside stars.

....

....

....
[2 marks]

1.4 Betelgeuse is another star in the Milky Way.

Betelgeuse is a red super giant star. Eventually the star will become a supernova.

Which of the following could Betelgeuse eventually become?

Tick **two** boxes.

☐ black hole

☐ white dwarf

☐ protostar

☐ neutron star

☐ black dwarf

[2 marks]

Most galaxies appear to be moving away from the Milky Way galaxy.
The light we see from them is red-shifted.

1.5 What is meant by red-shift?
Tick **one** box.

☐ The wavelength of the light has increased.

☐ The wavelength of the light has decreased.

☐ The speed of the light has increased.

☐ The speed of the light has decreased.

[1 mark]

Turn over for the next question

2 **Figure 1** shows a bar magnet.
The bar magnet is surrounded by a magnetic field.

2.1 Draw lines on **Figure 1** to show the shape and direction of the magnetic field surrounding the magnet.

Figure 1

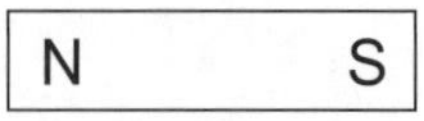

| N | S |

[3 marks]

2.2 State where the magnetic field of a bar magnet is strongest.

....
[1 mark]

An unmagnetised piece of iron is placed near the north pole of the magnet.
The north pole attracts the piece of iron.

2.3 Explain why the north pole of the magnet attracts the iron.

....

....

....
[2 marks]

2.4 State the equation that links work done, force and distance.

....
[1 mark]

The piece of iron moves 15 cm towards the north pole.
The average force on the piece of iron is 0.80 N.

2.5 Calculate the work done by the magnet on the iron.

....

....

Work done = ... J

[2 marks]

2.6 Describe the force experienced by the same piece of iron when it is placed near the south pole of the magnet.

....

[1 mark]

Iron is used to make transformers.

2.7 Describe the structure of a basic transformer.

....

....

[2 marks]

2.8 Describe how a step-up transformer differs from a step-down transformer in both its structure and function.

....

....

....

....

....

[2 marks]

Turn over for the next question

3 **Figure 2** shows a picture of a ripple tank. The ripples on the water form shadows on the floor. The size of the shadows is the same as the size of the ripples. The signal generator can be used to set the frequency of the ripples to a known value.

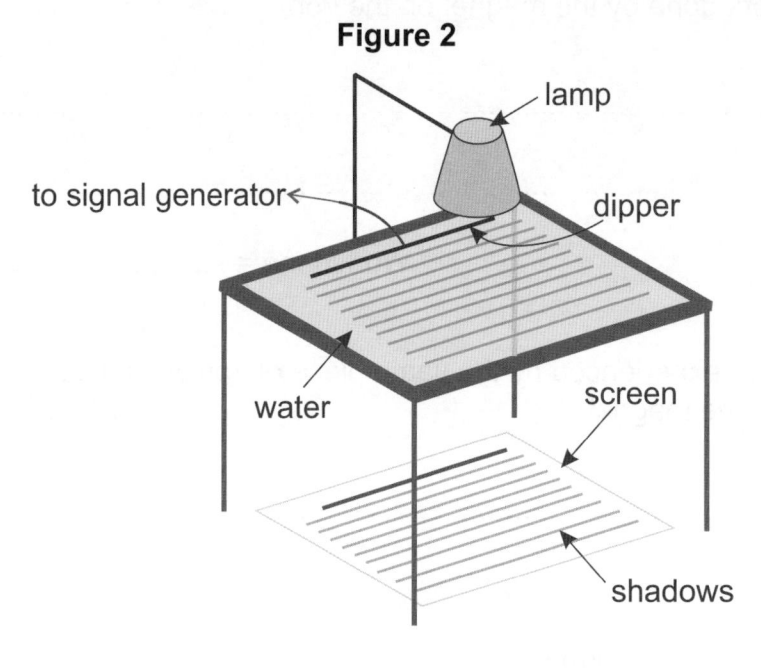

Figure 2

3.1 Describe a method to measure the speed of the ripples.
Your method should include how to ensure accurate measurements are taken.

....

....

....

....

....

....

....

....

[6 marks]

A student investigates how the speed of the ripples depends on the depth of the water.

3.2 State **one** variable that will need to be controlled in this investigation.

....

[1 mark]

The student's results are shown in **Table 1**.

Table 1

Water depth in cm	Speed in m/s
1	0.10
2	0.14
3	0.17
4	0.20
5	0.22

She draws the graph shown in **Figure 3**. Two data points are missing.

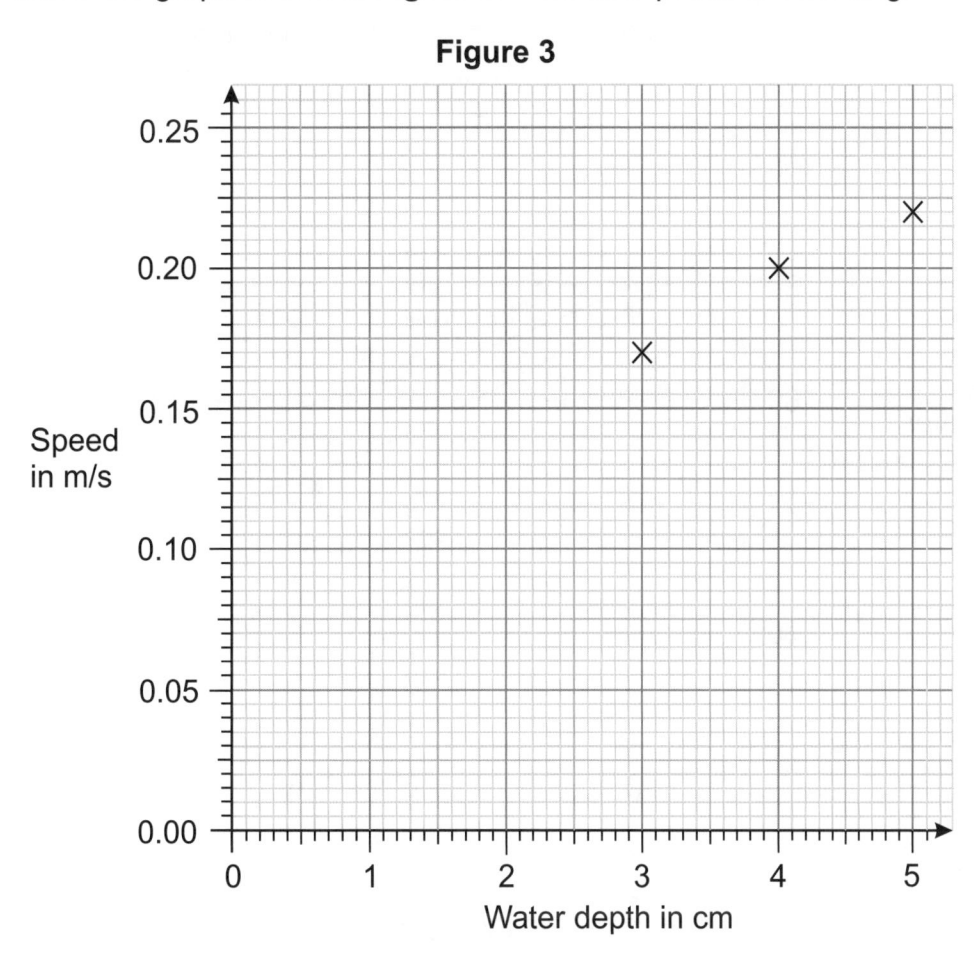

Figure 3

3.3 Complete **Figure 3** using data from **Table 1**.
Draw a line of best fit for the data.

[2 marks]

3.4 Describe the relationship between the depth of the water and the speed of the ripples.

....

....

....

[2 marks]

Turn over for the next question

Turn over ▶

4 A student is investigating two teapots, as shown in **Figure 4**.
One teapot has a white surface. The other teapot has a black surface.
The teapots are otherwise identical.

Figure 4

The student fills each teapot with 1 litre of hot water from a kettle.
He then plots a graph of the water temperature against time, shown in **Figure 5**.

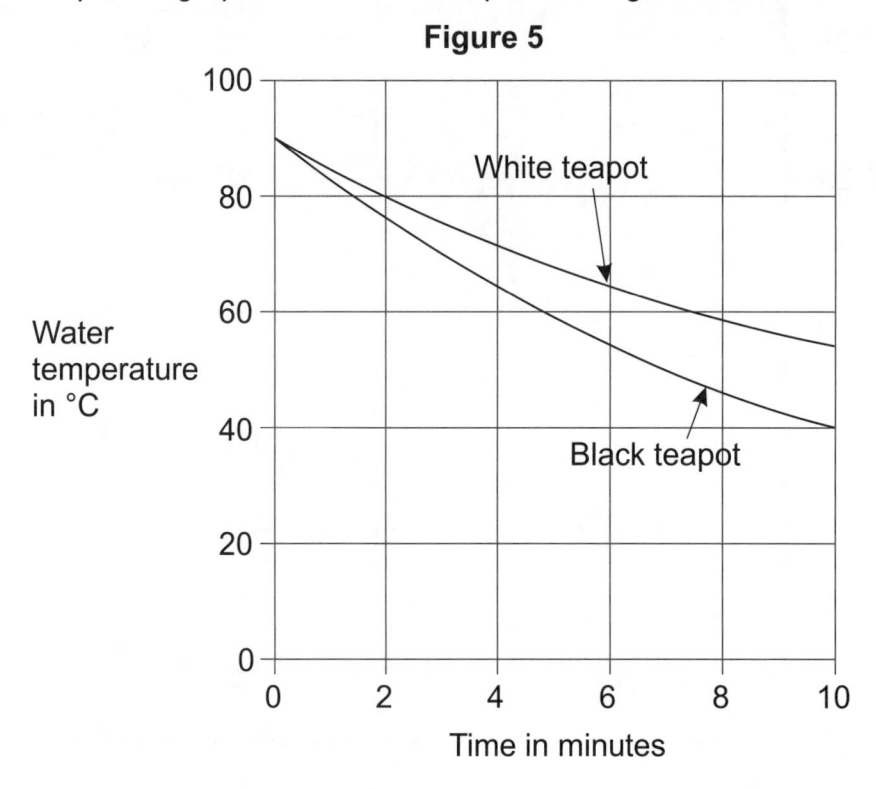

Figure 5

4.1 Describe and explain the results shown by **Figure 5**.
You should refer to energy transfers in your answer.

....

....

....

....

....
[4 marks]

After one hour, the water in both teapots has cooled down to room temperature. The water in both teapots then remains at a constant temperature.

4.2 Which of these statements is true for both teapots after 1 hour?
Tick **one** box.

☐ There is no energy transfer between the teapots and the surroundings.

☐ The black teapot is absorbing radiation at the same rate as the white teapot.

☐ Each teapot is absorbing radiation at the same rate as it is emitting it.

☐ Each teapot is absorbing radiation faster than it is emitting it.

[1 mark]

The student replaces the water in each teapot with cold water.
The initial water temperature of the water in both teapots is the same.

The student measures the temperature of the water in each teapot every 5 minutes. **Figure 6** is a graph showing how the water temperature for the white teapot varies with time.

4.3 Sketch a graph on **Figure 6** to show how the temperature of the water in the black teapot may have changed with time.

Figure 6

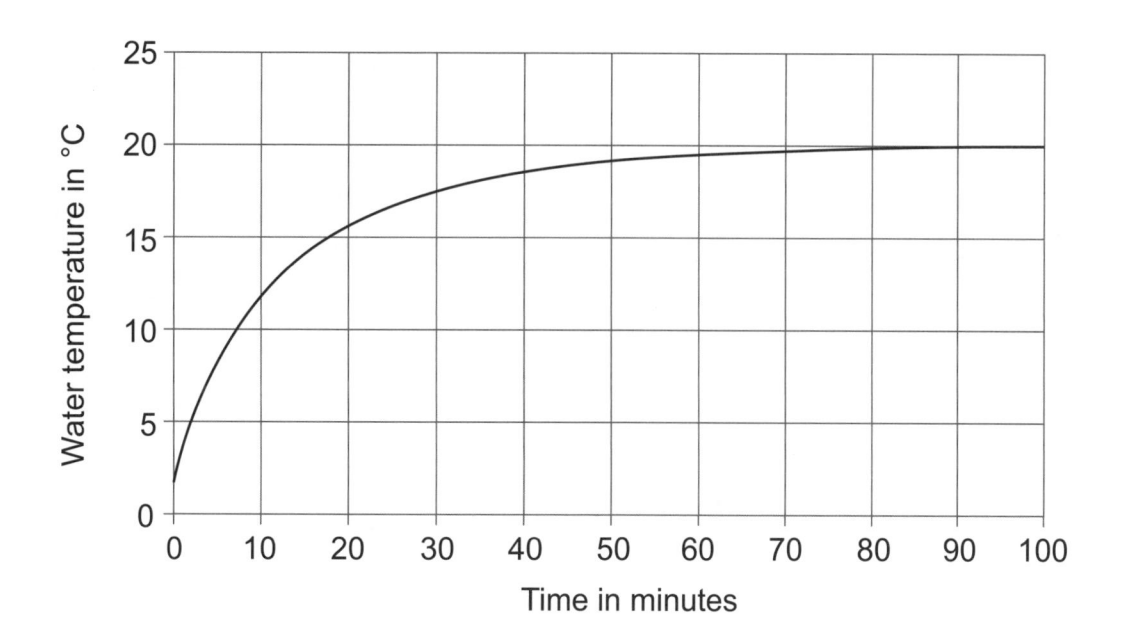

[3 marks]

Question 4 continues on the next page

Turn over ▶

The student says, "The black teapot is not a perfect black body."

4.4 State what is meant by a perfect black body.

....

....

[1 mark]

5 A footballer kicks a football against a wall, as shown in **Figure 7**.
The footballer stands 4 m away from the wall.
The football hits the wall and rebounds back towards the footballer.
The football has a mass of 400 g.

Figure 7

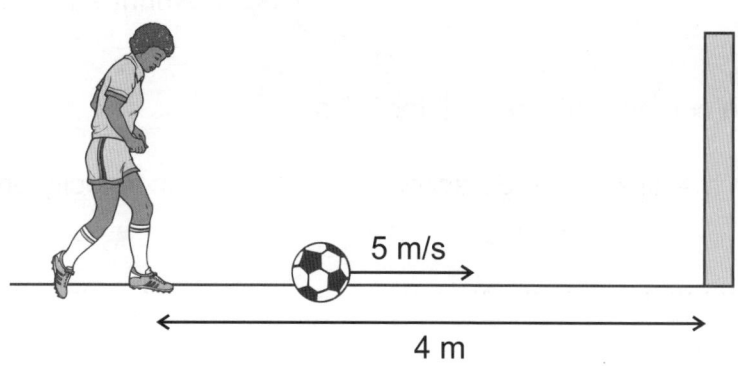

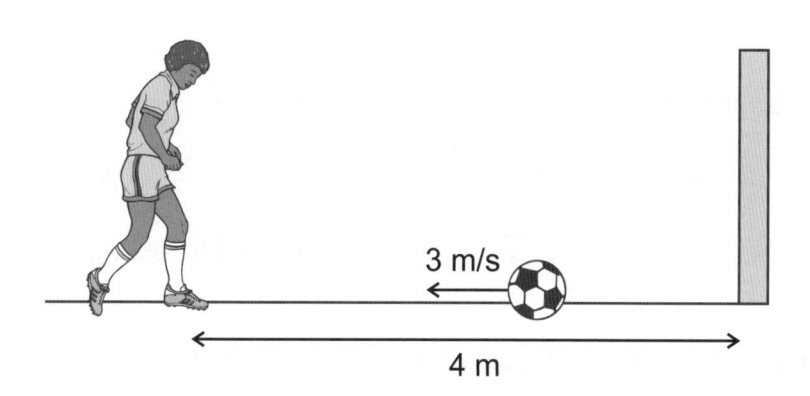

Table 2 compares the speed and velocity of the football:

Table 2

	Speed in m/s	Velocity in m/s
Before hitting the wall	5	5 →
After hitting the wall	3	3 ←

5.1 State what is represented by the arrows in **Table 2**.
Explain why they are not included in the column for speed.

....

....
[2 marks]

Question 5 continues on the next page

Turn over ▶

5.2 After rebounding off the wall, the football ends up where it started. Determine the size of the displacement of the football.

....

Displacement = ... m

[1 mark]

The football was in contact with the wall for 0.2 s.

5.3 State the equation that links average acceleration, change in velocity and time taken.

....

[1 mark]

5.4 Calculate the size of the average acceleration of the football when it was in contact with the wall.

....

....

Acceleration = ... m/s²

[2 marks]

5.5 Calculate the size of the average force the wall exerted on the football.

....

....

....

Force = ... N

[3 marks]

6 Lenses are used in glasses to correct vision problems.
One type of lens is shown in **Figure 8**.

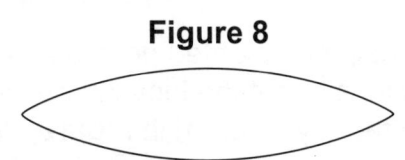

Figure 8

6.1 State the type of lens shown in **Figure 8**.

....
[1 mark]

A student conducts an experiment to measure the magnification of a lens.
One at a time, he places objects of different heights at the same position in front of the lens. He uses a ruler to measure the height of each object and the height of the corresponding image produced by the lens. **Figure 9** is a graph of his results.

Figure 9

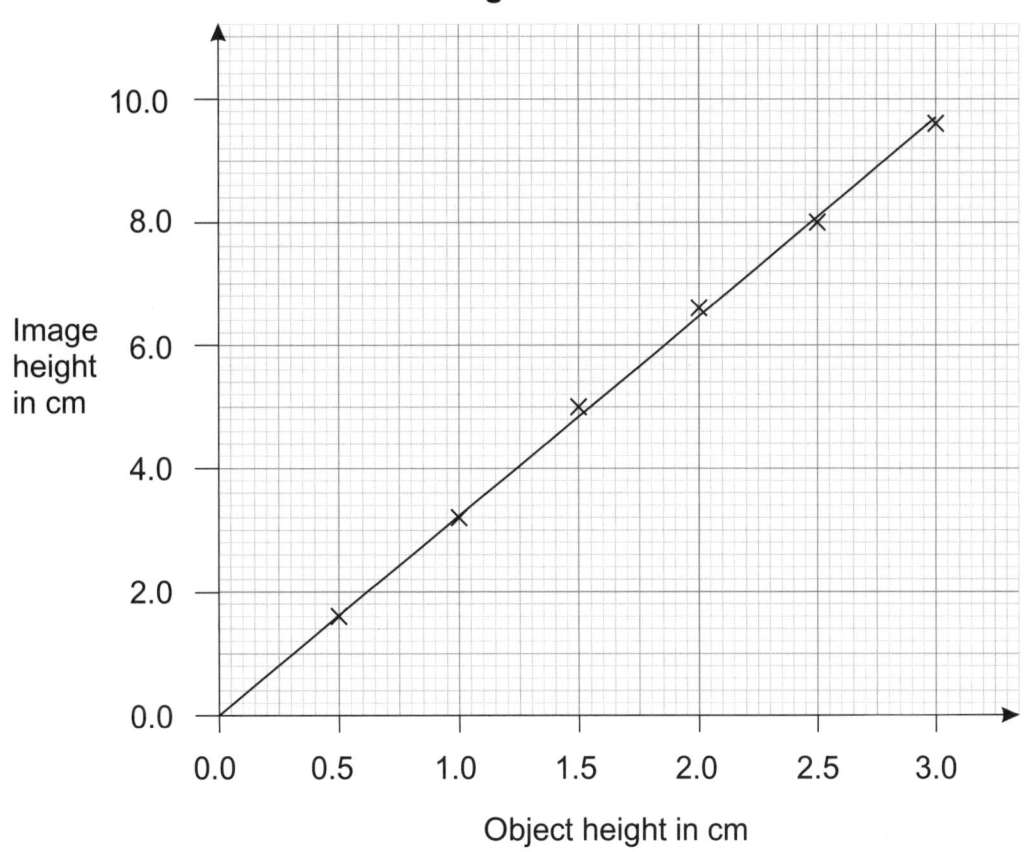

6.2 Calculate the magnification of the lens.
Give your answer to two significant figures.

....

....

Magnification = ...
[3 marks]

Question 6 continues on the next page

Some people are nearsighted. This means that nearby objects are in focus, but more distant objects are out of focus and look blurry.

6.3 Explain how concave lenses help nearsighted people to see more clearly. Your answer should include ideas about the location of the image formed and the type of the image. Complete the ray diagram in **Figure 10** as part of your answer.

Figure 10

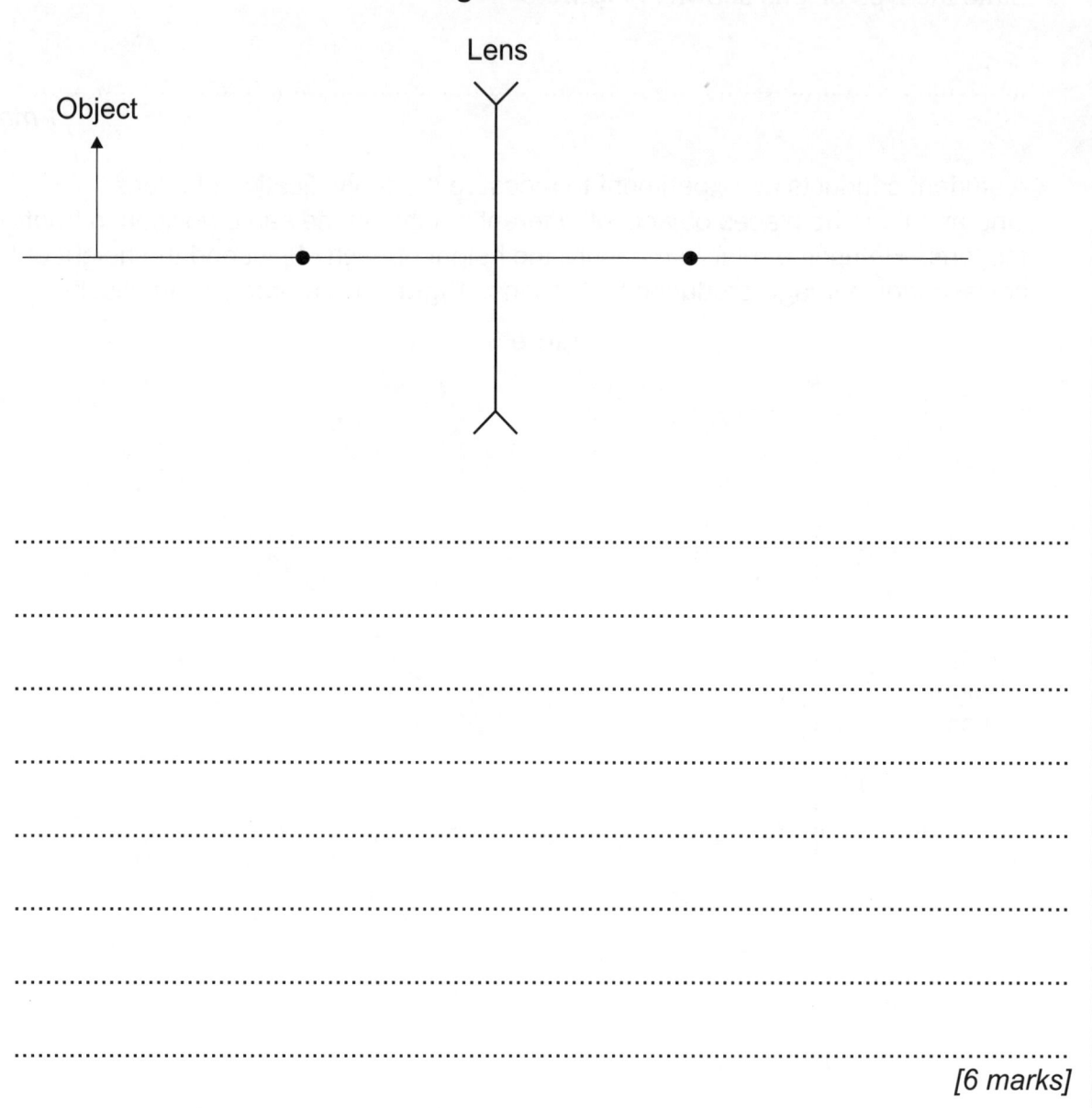

....

....

....

....

....

....

....

[6 marks]

7 A teacher shines a laser into a glass block.
Figure 11 is a ray diagram showing the laser light as it enters the block.

Figure 11

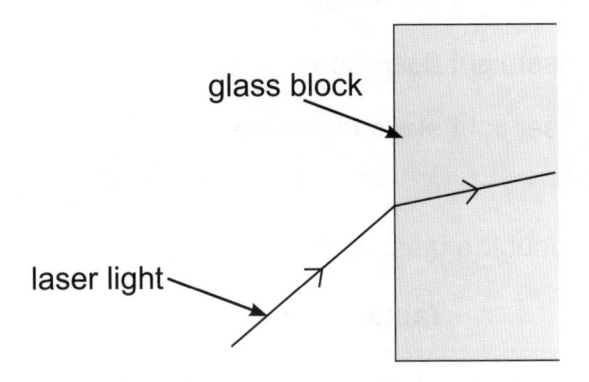

7.1 Name the effect shown by the path of the laser light in **Figure 11**.

....
[1 mark]

7.2 Give **one** safety precaution that the teacher should take when using the laser.

....

....
[1 mark]

Figure 12 shows an incomplete wave front diagram of the laser light passing from the air into the glass block.

7.3 Complete **Figure 12** by drawing the wave fronts inside the glass block.

Figure 12

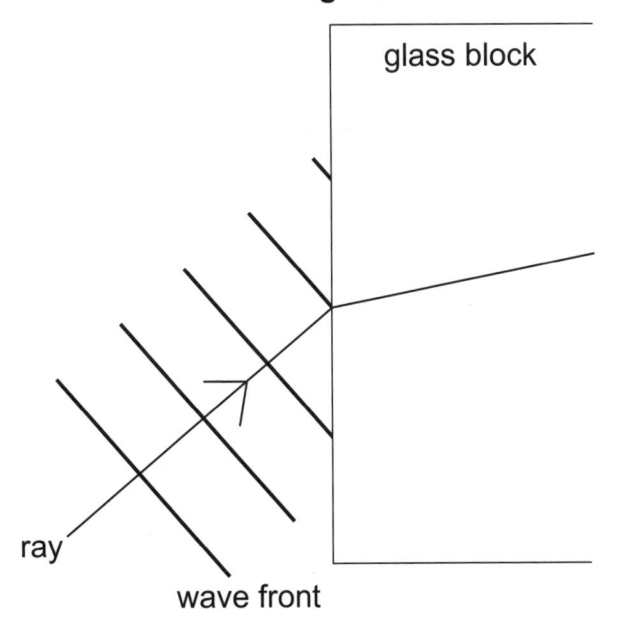

[2 marks]

Question 7 continues on the next page   **Turn over ▶**

7.4 Which of the following statements is true for the laser light as it passes into the glass block?
Tick **one** box.

☐ The frequency of the laser light increases.
☐ The frequency of the laser light decreases.
☐ The frequency of the laser light stays the same.

[1 mark]

7.5 Table 3 shows some data about the laser light.

Table 3

Wavelength outside the glass block	7.0×10^{-7} m
Speed outside the glass block	3.0×10^{8} m/s
Speed inside the glass block	2.0×10^{8} m/s

Calculate the wavelength of the laser light when it is inside the glass block.

....

....

....

....

Wavelength = ... m
[4 marks]

Turn over for the next question

8 A wooden cube is placed in a container of water. The cube floats on the surface.

8.1 The cube has a weight of 980 N.
State the size of the upthrust force acting on the cube.

Upthrust = ... N
[1 mark]

The cube is then held fully submerged in the water as shown in **Figure 13**.
The length of each side of the wooden cube is 0.05 m.

Figure 13

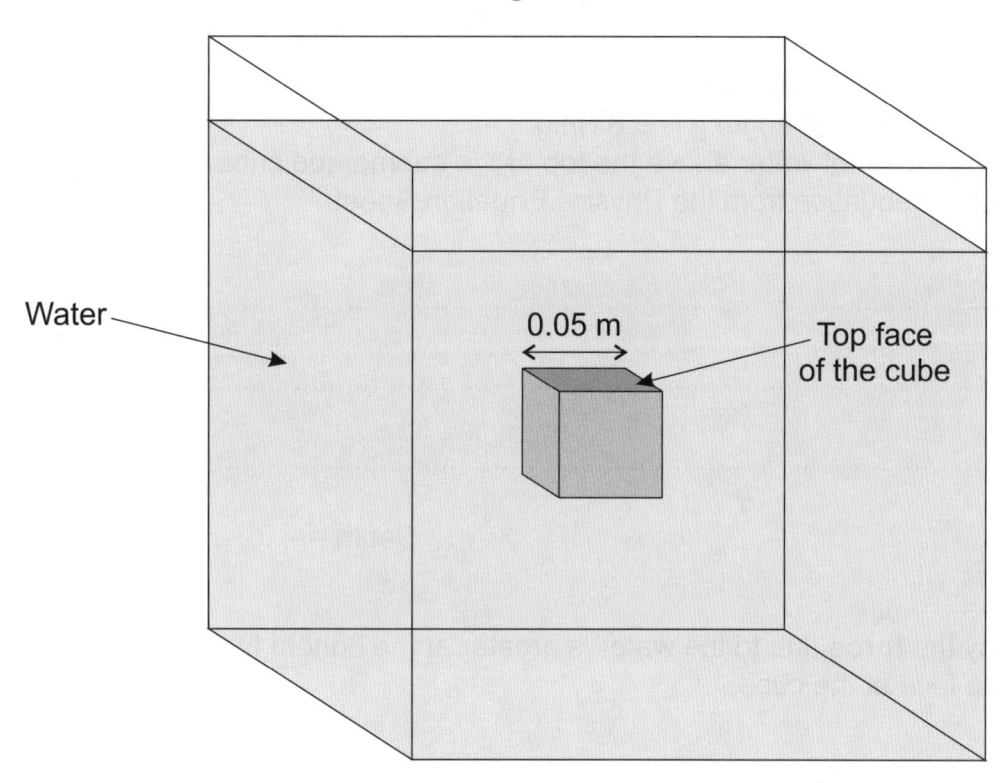

8.2 The water exerts forces on the cube. Draw an arrow on **Figure 13** to show the direction of the force acting on the left-hand side of the cube.
[1 mark]

Question 8 continues on the next page

Turn over ▶

The pressure due to the water on the top face of the submerged cube is 1470 Pa.

8.3 Calculate the force due to the water on the top face of the cube.

The length of each side of the cube is 0.1 m.

Force = ... N

[3 marks]

8.4 The density of water is 1000 kg/m³.
The gravitational field strength g is 9.8 N/kg.
Calculate the height of water above the top of the submerged cube.
Use the correct equation from the Physics Equation Sheet.

Depth = ... m

[2 marks]

8.5 Explain why the **force** due to the water is greater at the bottom face of the cube than the top face of the cube.

[2 marks]

9 Figure 14 is a speed-time graph of an ice hockey player during the first minute of a game.

Figure 14

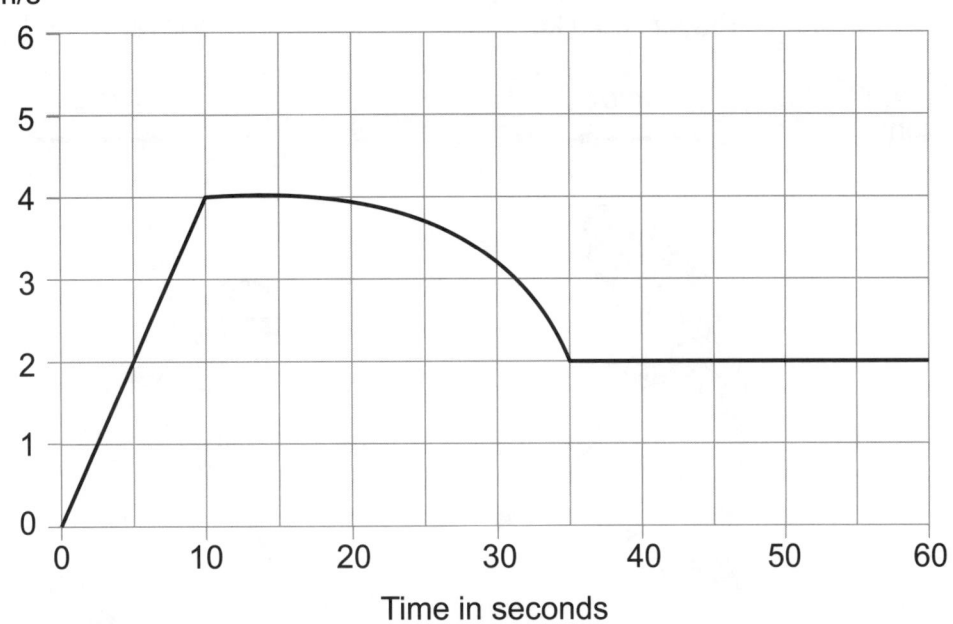

Speed in m/s vs Time in seconds. The speed increases linearly from 0 to 4 m/s between 0 and 10 seconds, remains at approximately 4 m/s until about 15 seconds, then curves downward to 2 m/s at 35 seconds, and remains constant at 2 m/s until 60 seconds.

9.1 Use **Figure 14** to describe the motion of the player and determine the distance she travels during the first minute of the game.

....

....

....

....

....

....

....

[5 marks]

Question 9 continues on the next page

Turn over ▶

Figure 15 shows the velocities of two ice hockey players before and after they collide during the game.

Figure 15

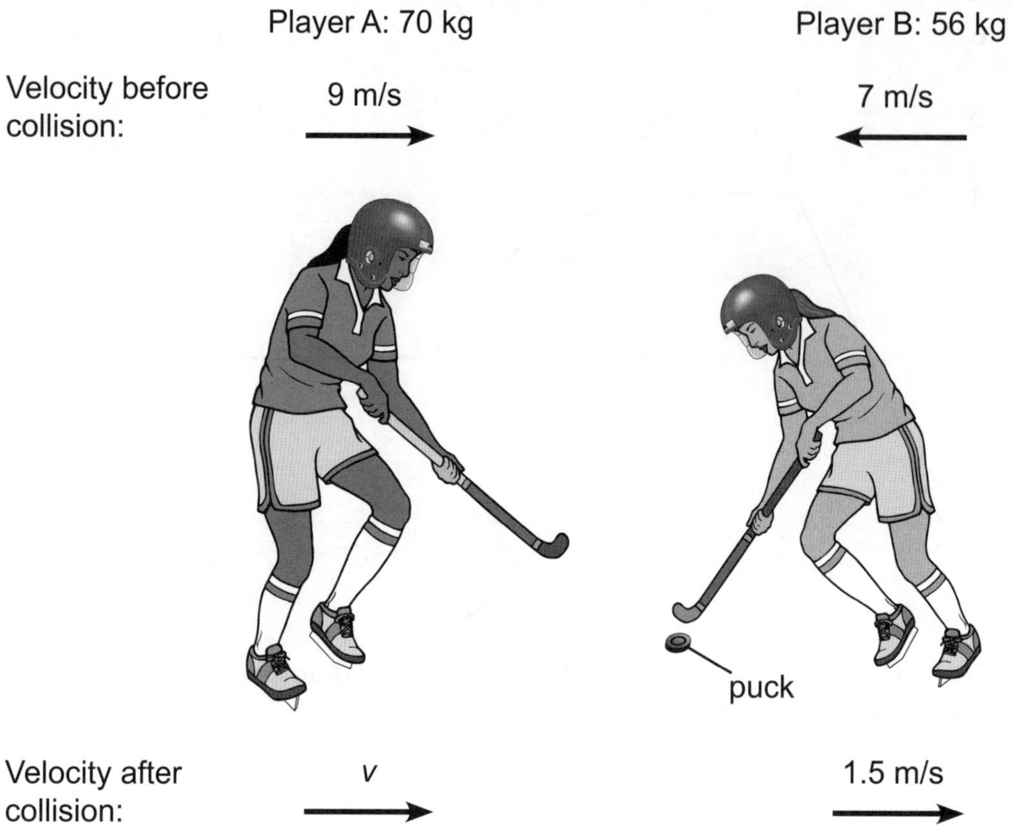

Player A: 70 kg Player B: 56 kg

Velocity before collision: 9 m/s →   7 m/s ←

puck

Velocity after collision: v →   1.5 m/s →

9.2 Calculate the value of v, the speed of player A after the collision.

....

....

....

....

Speed = ... m/s
[4 marks]

During the ice hockey game, two players try to hit the puck with their sticks. Both sticks hit the puck at the same time.

Figure 16 shows the forces that are exerted on the puck.

Figure 16

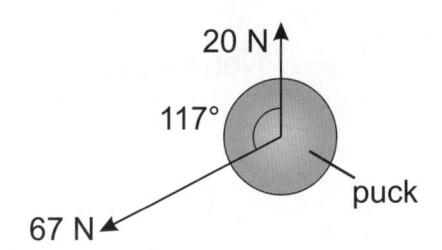

20 N
117°
67 N
puck

9.3 Use the squared grid below to calculate the magnitude of the resultant force.

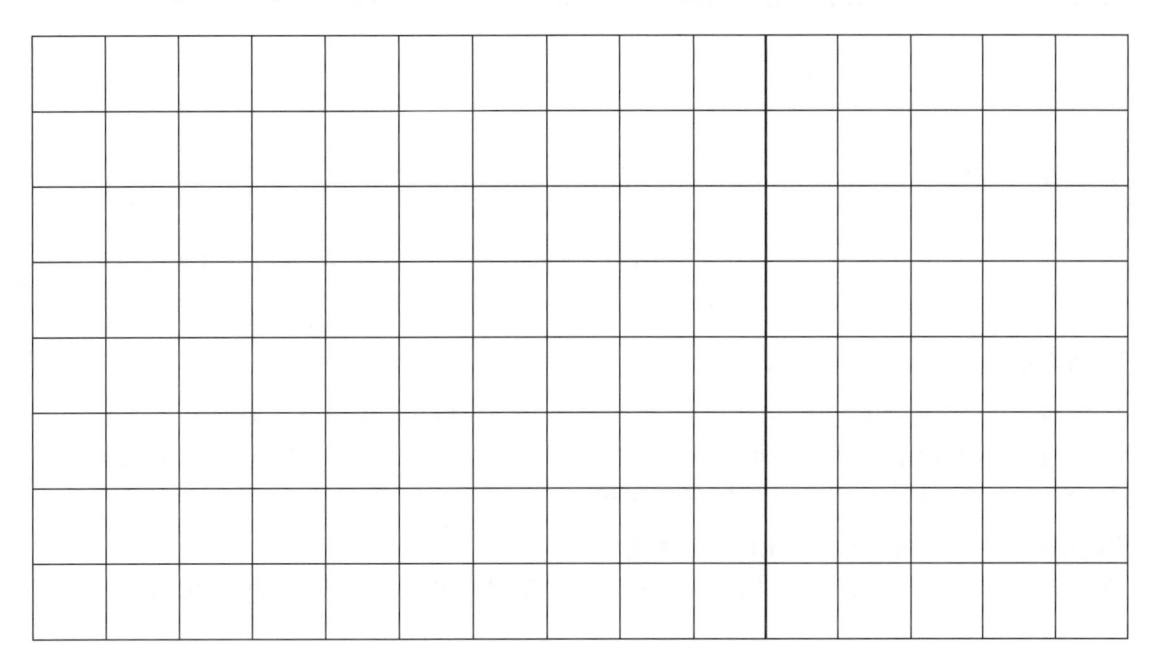

....

....

....

Resultant force = ... N

[3 marks]

Turn over for the next question

Turn over ▶

10 A playground has a seesaw designed for a single child, shown by **Figure 17**.
The child sits on one side of the pivot.
On the other side of the pivot there is a spring.

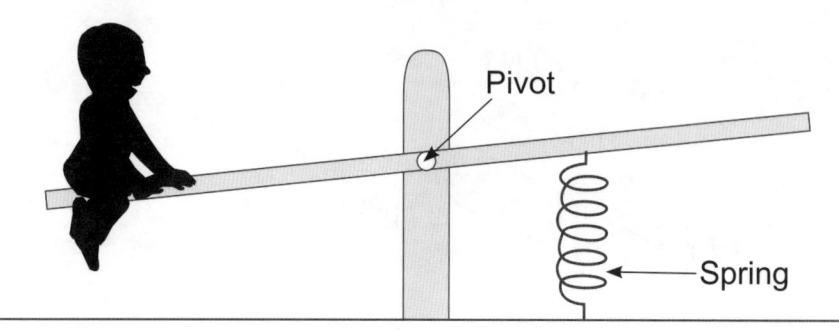

Figure 17

10.1 Explain how the spring helps the child to bounce up and down on the seesaw.

....

....

....
[2 marks]

10.2 Child A gets onto the seesaw.

Her weight exerts an anticlockwise moment of 150 Nm on the seesaw.
When the seesaw has rebalanced, the spring is extended by a total of 0.15 m.
The spring is 0.20 m away from the pivot.

Calculate the spring constant of the spring.
You can assume extension remains directly proportional to the force throughout.

....

....

....

....

Spring constant = ... N/m
[4 marks]

10.3 Calculate how much the spring is extended when 225 J is stored in its elastic potential energy store.
Use the correct equation from the Physics Equation Sheet.

....

....

....

....

Extension = ... m
[3 marks]

END OF QUESTIONS

GCSE Physics Equation Sheet

$p = h\rho g$	p pressure due to a column of liquid h height of column ρ density of liquid g gravitational field strength
$v^2 - u^2 = 2as$	v final velocity u initial velocity a acceleration s distance
$F = \dfrac{m\Delta v}{\Delta t}$	F force $m\Delta v$ change in momentum Δt time taken
$E_e = \tfrac{1}{2}ke^2$	E_e elastic potential energy k spring constant e extension
$\Delta E = mc\Delta\theta$	ΔE change in thermal energy m mass c specific heat capacity $\Delta\theta$ change in temperature
period = $\dfrac{1}{\text{frequency}}$	
magnification = $\dfrac{\text{image height}}{\text{object height}}$	
$F = BIl$	F force on a current-carrying conductor (at right angles to the field) B magnetic flux density I current l length
$E = mL$	E thermal energy for a change of state m mass L specific latent heat
$\dfrac{V_p}{V_s} = \dfrac{n_p}{n_s}$	V_p potential difference across primary coil V_s potential difference across secondary coil n_p number of turns in primary coil n_s number of turns in secondary coil
$V_s I_s = V_p I_p$	V_s potential difference across secondary coil I_s current in secondary coil V_p potential difference across primary coil I_p current in primary coil
For gases: pV = constant	p pressure V volume

CGP

GCSE AQA
Physics
For the Grade 9-1 Course

Practice Exam Papers
Instructions & Answer Book

Higher Tier

Pack Two

Inch-perfect exam practice from CGP!

You can't bluff your way through AQA's Grade 9-1 GCSE Physics exams.
No chance. What you need is a way of making sure you're 100% prepared.

That's where this brilliant pack from CGP comes in. It contains two full sets of realistic mock exams, so you get used to tackling the types of questions examiners love to ask — all in the comfort of your own home / classroom / private jet.

We've also included full answers and mark schemes for all the papers, so it's easy to check how you're getting on. You'll be ready for anything when the real exams roll around.

What to Expect in The Exams

1) Topics are Covered in Different Papers

For AQA GCSE Physics, you'll sit two exam papers at the end of your course.

Paper	Time	No. of marks	Specification Topics Assessed
1	1 hr 45 mins	100	1, 2, 3 and 4
2	1 hr 45 mins	100	5, 6, 7 and 8

You're expected to know the basic concepts of physics in both papers.

2) You'll be Tested on your Maths...

At least 30% of the total marks for AQA GCSE Physics come from questions on the maths skills you've used in the course. You'll be expected to calculate the mean and range for a set of data, so make sure you know how to do it for your exam.

3) ...and on your Practical Skills

- AQA GCSE Physics contains ten required practical activities that you'll do during the course — but you can also be asked about them in the exams.
- At least 15% of the total marks will be from questions testing practical skills.
- For example, you might be asked to comment on the design of an experiment (the apparatus and methods), make predictions, analyse or interpret results... Pretty much anything to do with planning and carrying out the investigations.

You could be asked about other practical activities as well. So you'll need to be able to apply the skills you've learnt for the required practicals to other experiments.

Marking Your Papers

- Do a complete exam set (Paper 1 and Paper 2).
- Use the answers and mark scheme in this booklet to mark each exam paper.
- Write down your mark for each paper in the table below — each paper is worth 100 marks.
- Find your total for the whole exam (out of a maximum of 200 marks) by adding up your marks from both papers.
- Follow the instructions below to estimate your grade.

	Paper 1	Paper 2	Total mark	Grade
SET A				
SET B				

Estimating Your Grade

- If you want to get a **rough idea** of the grade you're working at, we suggest you compare the **total mark** you got in **each set** to the latest set of grade boundaries.
- Grade boundaries are set for each individual exam, so they're likely to **change** from year to year. You can find the latest set of grade boundaries by going to **www.cgpbooks.co.uk/gcsegradeboundaries**
- Jot down the marks required for each grade in the table below so you don't have to refer back to the website. Use these marks to **estimate your grade**. If you're borderline, don't push yourself up a grade — the real examiners won't.

Total mark required for each grade						
Grade	9	8	7	6	5	4
Total mark out of 200						

- Remember, this will only be a **rough guide**, and grade boundaries will be different for different exams, but it should help you to see how you're getting on.

Published by CGP

Contributors: Jonathon Grange, Mark Edwards.

Editors: Sarah Armstrong, Duncan Lindsay, Ethan Starmer-Jones, Charlotte Whiteley, Sarah Williams.

Proofreaders: Mark Edwards, Matthew Benyohai.

Many thanks to Ana Pungartnik for the copyright research.

Clipart from Corel®
Printed by Elanders Ltd, Newcastle upon Tyne.

Text, design, layout and original illustrations
© Coordination Group Publications Ltd. (CGP) 2017
All rights reserved.

Photocopying more than one section of this book is not permitted, even if you have a CLA licence.
Extra copies are available from CGP with next day delivery • 0800 1712 712 • www.cgpbooks.co.uk

Answers

Set A — Paper 1

1.1 Because the resistance of a resistor changes with temperature, and the resistance of a resistor affects the current through it *[1 mark]*.

1.2 E.g. turn off the circuit between recordings (to prevent the resistor heating up due to the current flowing through it) / keep the range of currents low (to prevent the resistor heating up due to the current flowing through it) *[1 mark]*.

1.3 potential difference = current × resistance / $V = IR$ *[1 mark]*

1.4 Select pair of points from line best fit:
e.g. $V = 4.5$ V, $I = 0.75$ A
So $R = \dfrac{V}{I} = \dfrac{4.5}{0.75} = 6\ \Omega$
[2 marks for correct answer, otherwise 1 mark for correct substitution]

1.5 The resistor is ohmic because the graph is linear. *[1 mark]*

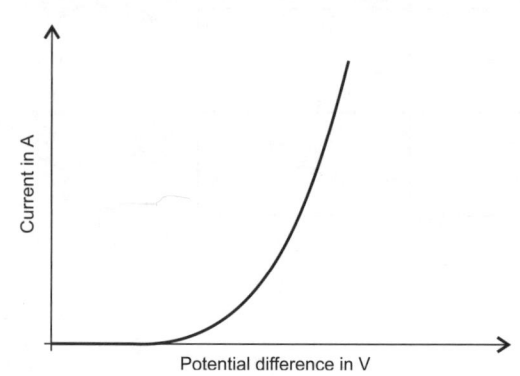

1.6
[Graph: Current in A (y-axis) vs Potential difference in V (x-axis), curve increasing exponentially]
[1 mark]

2.1 Energy is transferred mechanically from the chemical energy stores of the people's muscles *[1 mark]* to the kinetic energy store of the car *[1 mark]*.

2.2 gravitational potential energy = mass × gravitational field strength × height / $E_g = mgh$ *[1 mark]*

2.3 $E_g = 1200 \times 9.8 \times 5.0$
   $= 58\ 800$ J ($= 59\ 000$ J (to 2 s.f.))
[2 marks for correct answer, otherwise 1 mark for correct substitution]

2.4 E.g. some would have been transferred to thermal energy stores (due to work done against friction/resistive forces) *[1 mark]*

3.1 An alternating potential difference is constantly changing direction/the positive and negative ends keep swapping *[1 mark]* while a direct potential difference is always in the same direction *[1 mark]*.

3.2 230 V *[1 mark]*

3.3 A connection between the live wire and the earth wire is dangerous because it creates a low resistance path to the earth *[1 mark]*. This causes a large current to flow through the wires, which can cause a large heating effect and may result in a fire *[1 mark]*.

3.4 The network of cables and transformers which connects power stations to consumers *[1 mark]*.

3.5 Electricity in the national grid has a very high power. Power = current × potential difference, so transmitting electricity at a relatively small potential difference of 230 V would require a very large current to flow through the wires in the national grid *[1 mark]*. The larger the current, the more energy is wasted from the wires through heating *[1 mark]*. So electricity is transmitted at a higher potential difference, so that the same power can be delivered using a lower current and less energy is wasted *[1 mark]*.

3.6 A (step-down) transformer *[1 mark]*.

4.1 the nucleus *[1 mark]*

4.2 How to grade your answer:
Level 0: There is no relevant information. *[No marks]*
Level 1: There is a brief description of placing a material between the Geiger-Müller detector and a source and measuring a count rate in order to identify the type of radiation emitted by the source. *[1 to 2 marks]*
Level 2: There is a description of an experiment which could be carried out to determine the type of radiation emitted by a source, using the equipment shown. *[3 to 4 marks]*
Level 3: There is a clear and detailed description of an experiment which could be carried out to determine the type of radiation emitted by each source, using the equipment shown. *[5 to 6 marks]*

Here are some points your answer may include:
Set up the Geiger-Müller detector and counter.
Before placing any of the sources near the detector, record the background count rate.
For each radioactive source:
1. Place a source at a set distance, e.g. 10 cm, from the Geiger-Müller detector.
2. Record the number of counts over a time interval (e.g. 1 minute). Use this to work out the count rate in counts per second by dividing the number of counts by the number of seconds.
3. Place the sheet of card halfway between the Geiger-Müller detector and the source, and record the count rate.
4. Replace the card with the aluminium sheet, and record the count rate.
5. Replace the aluminium with the lead sheet, and record the count rate.

Compare the count rates recorded from each source.
If the count rate from the source is much lower/decreases to close to the background level after the card has been placed between the source and the detector, the source emits alpha radiation.
If the count rate from the source does not change much when the card is placed between the source and the detector, but is much lower/decreases to close to the background level after the aluminium is used, the source emits beta radiation.
If the count rate from the source does not change much when the aluminium is placed between the source and the detector, but is much lower after the lead is used, the source emits gamma radiation.

4.3 E.g. it will reduce the risk of the students being contaminated by the sources / the students will be further from the sources than if they directly touched them, so they may be irradiated less by radiation from the sources *[1 mark]*.

4.4 E.g. Radioactive sources are being used in the classroom, which is adding to the level of background radiation already present in the classroom *[1 mark]*.

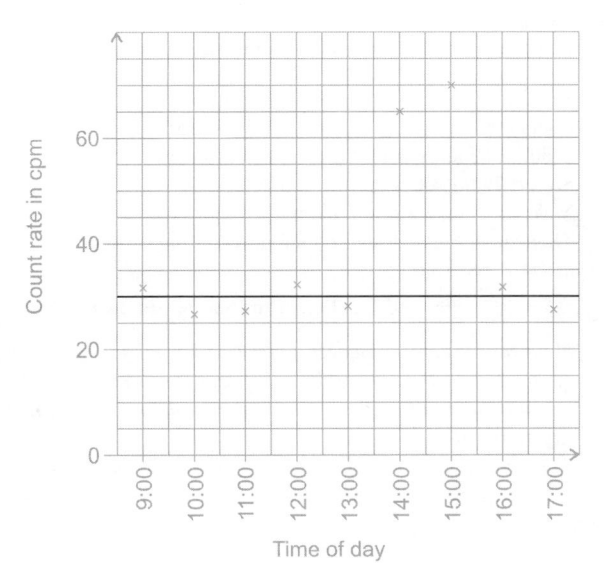

4.5

[1 mark]
This should be a line of best fit through all the points except those at 14:00 and 15:00. A horizontal line anywhere between 29 and 31 cpm will be accepted.

4.6 Background radiation is different in different locations, so the student cannot conclude that the reading of 50 cpm is not just due to background radiation *[1 mark]*.

4.7 Any two of: e.g. rocks / fall-out from nuclear weapons or nuclear accidents / industry / medicine *[1 mark]*.

5.1 $P = I^2R$ so $R = \dfrac{P}{I^2}$
$R = \dfrac{14.5}{(0.063)^2} = 3653.313...\ \Omega\ (= 3700\ \Omega\ \text{to 2 s.f.})$
[2 marks for correct answer, otherwise 1 mark for correct substitution]

5.2 Any two from: e.g. LEDs are more efficient than filament lamps, so waste less energy / LEDs have a lower input power than filament lamps, so would use less electricity and cost less to use / LEDs have a much longer lifetime than filament bulbs.
[2 marks — 1 mark for each sensible answer]

5.3 efficiency = $\dfrac{\text{useful power output}}{\text{total power input}}$
so total power input = $\dfrac{\text{useful power output}}{\text{efficiency}}$
useful power output = 3.75 W
efficiency = 5.0% = 0.050
total power input = $\dfrac{3.75}{0.050}$ = **75 W**
[3 marks for correct answer, otherwise 1 mark for correct rearrangement and 1 mark for correct substitution]

6.1 An isotope is an atom of an element with (the same number of protons but) a different number of neutrons (to another atom of that element) *[1 mark]*.

6.2

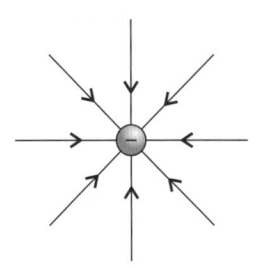

[1 mark for drawing radial field lines, 1 mark for drawing arrows pointing towards the charged sphere on every line]

6.3 The radon nucleus loses 2 protons and 2 neutrons (that are emitted as an alpha particle) *[1 mark]*.

6.4 How to grade your answer:
Level 0: There is no relevant information. *[No marks]*
Level 1: There is a suggestion of which isotope is best suited for use as a medical tracer, with a brief explanation of how it is suited to this use. *[1 to 2 marks]*
Level 2: There is a suggestion of which isotope is best suited for use as a medical tracer, with a clear and detailed explanation of how the properties of the isotope make it suited to this use. *[3 to 4 marks]*

Here are some points your answer may include:
Technetium-99m is best suited to use as a medical tracer.
Technetium-99m is a gamma source.
This means the radiation it emits is penetrating enough to escape from the human body, and be measured by a detector outside the body.
Technitium-99m's half-life is long enough that radiation will be emitted at detectable levels while it is in use.
Its half-life is also short enough that the patient will not be exposed to radiation for too long after it is used.
It also means the patient will not be radioactive for long after it is used, and so won't pose a risk to other people.

6.5 Any two from: e.g. so that they can be properly checked by other scientists by peer review *[1 mark]* / so that the potential benefits and risks of the treatment can be shared amongst the scientific community *[1 mark]* / so that other scientists can repeat the trial/test the claims *[1 mark]*.

7.1 $\rho = \dfrac{m}{V}$, so $V = \dfrac{m}{\rho}$
$V = \dfrac{3.0}{1.225} = $ **2.44897... m³ (= 2.4 m³ (to 2 s.f.))**
[3 marks for correct answer, otherwise 1 mark for correct rearrangement and 1 mark for correct substitution]

7.2 An increase in temperature causes an increase in pressure *[1 mark]*. This is because an increase in temperature means an increase in energy in the kinetic energy stores of the particles, so they move faster *[1 mark]*. This means they collide with the walls of the container with greater force, and more often (since the volume is fixed), and so the pressure is greater *[1 mark]*.

7.3 It is dangerous because the increase in pressure may be too much for the container, which may cause the container to rupture/explode *[1 mark]*.

7.4 The density doesn't change *[1 mark]* because the mass and volume of gas have both remained the same *[1 mark]*.

8.1 Readings vary between 1 Ω above and 1 Ω below the mean value *[1 mark]*. Therefore the uncertainty is ± 1 Ω *[1 mark]*.
Alternatively, the uncertainty can be calculated by dividing the range by two.

8.2

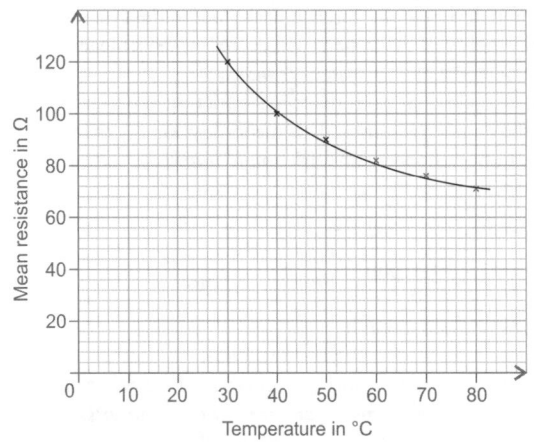

[1 mark for sensible, smooth, curved line of best fit, 2 marks for all points plotted correctly, otherwise 1 mark for at least two points plotted correctly]

8.3 Any two of: e.g. put the thermistor in an ice bath to decrease the temperature further / use a higher temperature of water to start with / use a different means of heating (e.g. an oven) which can reach a higher temperature.
[2 marks — 1 mark for each correct answer]

8.4 How to grade your answer:
Level 0: There is no relevant information. *[No marks]*
Level 1: There is a brief description of how the temperature of the room changed, and how you can tell this from the graph. *[1 to 2 marks]*
Level 2: There is a clear and detailed description of how the temperature of the room changed throughout the 24 hour period. There is a clear explanation of how these conclusions can be drawn from the graph.
[3 to 4 marks]
Here are some points your answer may include:
The resistance of the thermistor decreases with increasing temperature (as shown in Figure 8).
Since the potential difference is fixed, the lower the resistance, the more current flows.
So the higher the current shown on the graph, the higher the temperature.
From 10:00, the temperature of the room increased for three hours / until 13:00.
The temperature then remained constant for two hours / until 15:00.
The temperature then decreased for seven hours / until 22:00.
The temperature then remained constant for two hours / until 00:00.
It then decreased again for two hours / until 02:00, and then remained constant for another two hours / until 04:00.
From 04:00, the temperature of the room gradually increased again.

9.1 The water vapour particles will have a higher average kinetic energy than those of liquid water *[1 mark]*. When the lid of the cup is removed, water vapour escapes the system, so the molecules with the highest energy are removed from the system. This means the average kinetic energy of the system is now lower *[1 mark]*.

9.2 First find the mass of water vapour that escaped the cup:
$E = mL$, so $m = E \div L$
$m = 20\,300 \div 2\,257\,000 = 0.0089942...$ kg
Convert mass to g, $m = 0.0089942... \times 1000$
$= 8.9942...$ g
So the total mass left inside the cup is
$225 - 8.9942... = \mathbf{216.005...\ g\ (= 216\ g\ to\ 3\ s.f.)}$
[3 marks for correct answer, otherwise 1 mark for correct substitution, 1 mark for finding the total mass of the water vapour that escaped]

9.3 For a system to be a closed system, there can be no net change in total energy *[1 mark]*. The cardboard cup allows energy to be transferred to the surroundings / out of the system, and so the total energy of the system will decrease. This means it can't be considered a closed system *[1 mark]*.

10.1 Oil is a lubricant, so it reduces the friction between moving parts of the engine *[1 mark]*. This means less energy is lost by heating due to work done against friction *[1 mark]*.

10.2 $E_k = \frac{1}{2}mv^2$
Rearrange for speed, $v = \sqrt{\frac{2E_k}{m}}$
$v = \sqrt{\frac{2 \times 2\,400\,000}{750}} = \sqrt{6400} = 80$ m/s
Convert speed to km/h
$v = (80 \times 60 \times 60) \div 1000 = \mathbf{288\ km/h}$
[3 marks for correct answer, otherwise 1 mark for correct substitution and 1 mark for correct answer in m/s]

10.3 $E = mc\Delta\theta$
Rearrange for change in temperature, $\Delta\theta$:
$\Delta\theta = \frac{E}{mc}$
Energy transferred to thermal energy stores of brakes, E, is 80% of energy from the car's kinetic energy store.
So $E = 2\,400\,000 \times 0.8 = 1\,920\,000$ J
Mass of 1 brake disc = 1500 g = 1.5 kg
There are 4 brake discs, so total mass of brake discs,
$m = 4 \times 1.5 = 6.0$ kg
$\Delta\theta = \frac{1\,920\,000}{6.0 \times 600} = \mathbf{533.333...\ °C\ (= 530\ °C\ (to\ 2\ s.f.))}$
[4 marks for correct answer, otherwise 1 mark for calculation of energy transferred to thermal energy stores of brakes, 1 mark for calculation of total mass of brakes and 1 mark for correct substitution]
You could have also found the energy transferred by one brake and then substituted that energy and the mass of one brake into the specific heat capacity equation. You'd get a mark for dividing the energy by 4 rather than finding the total mass of the four brakes if you calculated the temperature change this way.

10.4 The engineers should use Set B, because they have a higher specific heat capacity *[1 mark]*, so they will have a smaller increase in temperature for the same transfer of energy, and will be less likely to get too hot and fail *[1 mark]*.

11.1 $E = Pt$ and $P = VI$, so need to find I through and V across motor.
Potential difference across motor = potential difference across bulb = potential difference of battery − potential difference across the resistor.
Potential difference across motor = 9.0 − 6.2
= 2.8 V
Current through motor = total current through circuit − current through bulb
= 0.40 − 0.15
= 0.25 A
Power is given by $P = VI$, so:
$P = 2.8 \times 0.25 = 0.7$ W
Energy transferred by the motor is given by $E = Pt$, so energy transferred in 30 s is:
$E = 0.7 \times 30$
$= \mathbf{21\ J}$
[5 marks for correct answer, otherwise 1 mark for correct potential difference across the motor, 1 mark for correct current through the motor, 1 mark for correct substitution to find power, 1 mark for correct substitution to find energy transferred.]

11.2 The potential difference across the motor is lower in Figure 14, since the motor shares the potential difference from the power supply with the other components, while the potential difference across it is equal to the potential difference across the power supply in Figure 15 *[1 mark]*. As $V = IR$, this means that the current must be lower through the motor in Figure 14 *[1 mark]*. Since both the current through and potential difference across the motor are lower in Figure 14, its power must be lower since $P = IV$ *[1 mark]*.

11.3 Because the resistance of a filament bulb increases with increasing potential difference *[1 mark]*.

Set A — Paper 2

1.1 Any two of: e.g. the student changed two variables at once (the angle and the ramp) *[1 mark]*. He should only change one variable so he can be sure which is causing any change in the results *[1 mark]*. / The student is calculating the average speed (from the time taken to travel down the ramp) instead of the speed at the bottom of the ramp *[1 mark]*. He should use a light gate to measure the speed of the trolley directly at the bottom of the ramp / find the time for the trolley to travel a set horizontal distance after it leaves the ramp and calculate the speed from this *[1 mark]*. / The stopwatch may give inaccurate results, as it is affected by human reaction times *[1 mark]*. He could use light gates to automatically record time values *[1 mark]*.

1.2 Weight = mass × gravitational field strength or $W = mg$ *[1 mark]*

1.3 $W = 0.40 \times 9.8 = 3.92$ N
$F = 0.5 \times W = 0.5 \times 3.92 =$ **1.96 N**
[2 marks for correct answer, otherwise 1 mark for calculating the weight.]

2.1 From 10 s to 12 s *[1 mark]*
A curve with a decreasing gradient on a distance-time graph shows deceleration.

2.2 Speed is given by the gradient of a distance-time graph.
Between 2 s and 10 s:
gradient = $\frac{\text{change in } y}{\text{change in } x} = \frac{42 - 2}{10 - 2} = \frac{40}{8} =$ **5 m/s**
[3 marks for correct answer, otherwise 1 mark for correct method of speed calculation and 1 mark for correctly reading distance and time values from the graph]

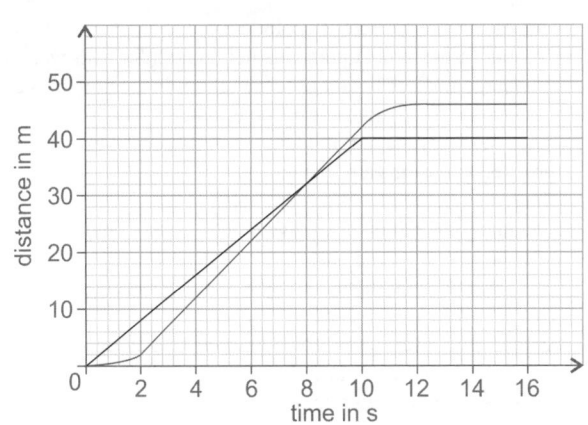

2.3
[1 mark for straight line drawn from the origin to 40 m at 10 s, 1 mark for horizontal line at 40 m from 10 s to 16 s]

2.4 Cyclist 1 overtakes Cyclist 2 when the distance-time graph of Cyclist 1 crosses over the distance-time graph of Cyclist 2. So Cyclist 1 overtakes Cyclist 2 at time = **8 s** *[1 mark]*
You'll get all the marks here as long as your answer is correct for the graph you drew in question part 2.3.

3.1 A scalar is a quantity which only has a size/magnitude, while a vector is a quantity that has both a size/magnitude and a direction *[1 mark]*.

3.2 The forces on the car are in equilibrium. *[1 mark]*

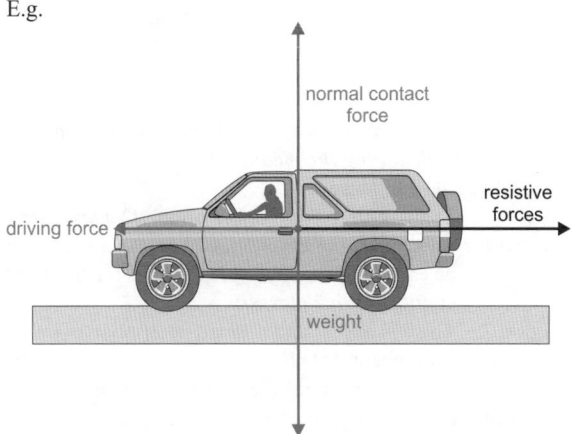

3.3 E.g.

[1 mark for line drawn pointing to the right that is longer than the driving force arrow]
The resistive forces are greater than the driving force, which causes a resultant force in the opposite direction to the direction of motion *[1 mark]*. Newton's second law says $F = ma$, and since the mass is constant, the acceleration of an object is proportional to the resultant force acting on it. So the car accelerates in the opposite direction to the direction of motion, which slows the car down *[1 mark]*.

3.4 Force = mass × acceleration / $F = ma$ *[1 mark]*

3.5 $a = \frac{F}{m} = \frac{1620}{1800} =$ **0.9 m/s²**
[2 marks for correct answer, otherwise 1 mark for correct substitution]

3.6 E.g. using a scale of 2 squares = 1 cm = 10 N

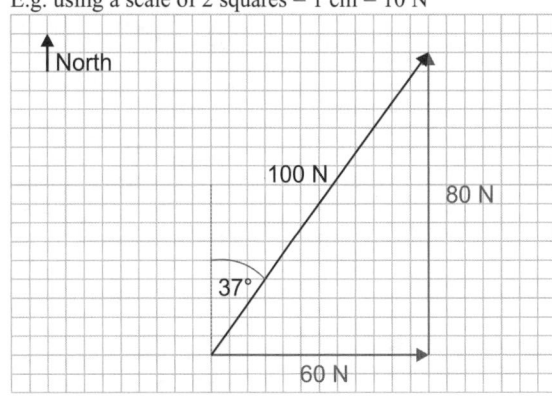

Length of resultant force line = 10 cm
So magnitude = 100 N
Direction = 37°
[1 mark for correct conversion of forces using a suitable scale factor, drawn correctly in a closed triangle, 1 mark for correctly measured and converted size of resultant force, 1 mark for correctly measured angle. Accept any values of resultant force between 95 N and 105 N and any direction between 35° and 39°.]

4.1 The colour an object appears is determined by the wavelengths/colours of visible light it reflects *[1 mark]*. The black flask appears black because it absorbs all wavelengths/colours of visible light *[1 mark]*. The white flask appears white because it reflects all wavelengths/colours of visible light equally *[1 mark]*.

4.2 The colour of the flasks *[1 mark]*

4.3 The final temperature / temperature change of the flask *[1 mark]*

4.4 E.g. starting temperature / size of flask / shape of flask / material of flask / distance of flask from heater / volume/mass of water in the flasks *[1 mark]*.

4.5 mean temperature of black flask at 5 minutes = $\frac{41+38+41}{3}$
$= \frac{120}{3}$
$= 40\ °C$
[2 marks for correct answer, otherwise 1 mark for correct method of calculating the mean]

4.6 How to grade your answer:
Level 0: There is no relevant information. *[No marks]*
Level 1: There is a brief description of an experiment that could be carried out to find which flask is the better infrared emitter. *[1 to 2 marks]*
Level 2: There is a clear and detailed description of an experiment that could be carried out to find which flask is the better infrared emitter. *[3 to 4 marks]*
Here are some points your answer may include:
Place each flask on a separate heat-proof mat.
Fill each flask with a fixed volume of hot water and seal the flask.
Make sure the water in each flask starts at the same temperature (e.g. 80 °C).
Compare the temperatures of each flask after a time interval.
The flask whose water temperature decreases more in a given time is the better emitter of infrared radiation because it has transferred away more energy by radiation and so cooled down more.

5.1 The image produced by a convex lens can be real or virtual. *[1 mark]*

5.2 focal length *[1 mark]*

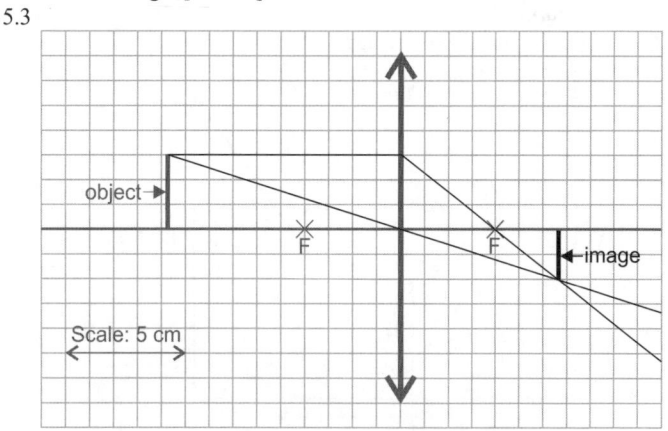

5.3

[1 mark for correctly drawn line passing through the principle focus, 1 mark for correctly drawn line passing through the middle of the lens, 1 mark for correctly drawn image]

5.4 magnification = $\frac{\text{image height}}{\text{object height}}$
image height = 2 squares = 2 cm
object height = 3 squares = 3 cm
magnification = $\frac{2}{3}$ = **0.6666... (= 0.67 (to 2 s.f.))**
[3 marks for answer between 0.6 and 0.8, otherwise 1 mark for correct measurement of heights and 1 mark for correct substitution]
You'll get the marks here as long as you correctly measure the image height from your ray diagram, and your answer is correct for this value.

6.1 E.g. iron / nickel / steel / cobalt *[1 mark]*

6.2 E.g. the Earth's core is magnetic so it has a magnetic field, and the magnetic compass needle aligns with the magnetic field of the Earth *[1 mark]*.

6.3 E.g. Another magnet/magnetic material is nearby *[1 mark]*

6.4 P-waves are longitudinal waves, while S-waves are transverse waves *[1 mark]*. P-waves can travel through solids and liquids, while S-waves can only travel through solids *[1 mark]*.

6.5 S-waves can travel through solids, but not liquids. S-waves are blocked by something in the core of the Earth, since they don't reach the other side. The inner core is solid, so layer Y must be liquid *[1 mark]*. Layer X must be solid, since S-waves can travel through it to reach over half of the Earth's surface *[1 mark]*.

7.1 The ISS has a faster orbital speed than the communications satellite, because its orbital radius is smaller *[1 mark]*.

7.2 Radiation dose is a measure of the risk of harm to a person's body from exposure to radiation *[1 mark]*

7.3 E.g. gamma rays can cause cancer/gene mutations *[1 mark]*.

7.4 A supernova is the explosion that occurs at the end of the red super giant stage of a star's life *[1 mark]*. After a supernova, either a neutron star *[1 mark]* or a black hole is left behind *[1 mark]*.

7.5 How to grade your answer:
Level 0: There is no relevant information. *[No marks]*
Level 1: There is a brief description of some stages in the life cycle of a star the size of the Sun. *[1 to 2 marks]*
Level 2: There is a description of each major stage in the life cycle of a star the size of the Sun. *[3 to 4 marks]*
Level 3: There is a clear and detailed description of the each stage in the life cycle of a star the size of the Sun. *[5 to 6 marks]*
Here are some points your answer may include:
The star initially forms from a nebula (a cloud of dust and gas) that is drawn together by the force of gravity.
This forms a protostar.
As the particles are drawn together, the protostar gets denser and hotter.
This causes the particles to collide more.
Eventually, the temperature gets hot enough for hydrogen nuclei to undergo nuclear fusion to form helium in the core of the protostar, and the protostar becomes a main sequence star.
When the star runs out of hydrogen in its core, it expands and turns red and forms a red giant.
The red giant then fuses larger nuclei.
Eventually the red giant star becomes unstable, and ejects its outer layer of dust and gas.
This leaves behind its incredibly hot and dense core.
This is a white dwarf star.
As the white dwarf cools down, it emits less energy, and eventually becomes a black dwarf star.

8.1 The generator is an alternator *[1 mark]*, since the direction of the potential difference changes *[1 mark]*.

8.2 For each rotation in an alternator, there is one positive and one negative potential difference peak. Each division is 1 second. There are 2 sets of positive and negative peaks in each division, so the number of rotations per second = **2**.
[2 marks for correct answer, otherwise 1 mark for correctly stating the number of peaks in each division]
Each rotation has a positive and negative peak because the direction of potential difference swaps every half turn. This is because the motion of the conductor with respect to the magnetic field swaps every half turn, so the direction of the potential difference swaps too.

8.3 $v = f\lambda$,
so $\lambda = \frac{v}{f} = \frac{3.00 \times 10^8}{39.2 \times 10^3}$ = **7653.06... m (= 7650 m (to 3 s.f.))**
[2 marks for correct answer, otherwise 1 mark for correct substitution]

8.4 $F = BIl$, so $I = \frac{F}{Bl}$
$I = \frac{0.880}{0.160 \times 10.4}$ = 0.5288... A = **0.529 A (to 3 s.f.)**
[3 marks for correct answer, otherwise 1 mark for correct substitution and 1 mark for the correct answer but not rounded to the correct number of significant figures]

9.1 $M = Fd$
moment due to ball 1 = 5.88 × 0.52 = 3.0576 Nm
moment due to ball 2 = 1.47 × 0.85 = 1.2495 Nm
Total anticlockwise moment = moment due to ball 1
                              + moment due to ball 2
                            = 3.0576 + 1.2495
                            = 4.3071 Nm
According to the principle of moments, for the plank to be balanced, the total anticlockwise moment has to equal the total clockwise moment.
So total clockwise moment = 4.3071 Nm
$M = Fd$, so $F = \frac{M}{d}$
$F = \frac{4.3071}{0.25} = \mathbf{17.2284 \text{ N} \ (= 17.2 \text{ N (to 3 s.f.)})}$
[5 marks for correct answer, otherwise 1 mark for correctly calculating the moment caused by one ball, 1 mark for calculating the total anticlockwise moment, 1 mark for applying the principle of moments and 1 mark for correct substitution]

9.2 Move the pivot along the plank so that the distance between the pivot and the force applied is smaller/the distance between the pivot and the balls is bigger *[1 mark]*. The side of the plank holding the balls travels further when the child pushes the right side down. So the balls move faster *[1 mark]*.

9.3 $v^2 - u^2 = 2as$
so $v = \sqrt{u^2 + 2as}$
Started at rest, so $u = 0$ m/s
$v = \sqrt{0^2 + (2 \times 9.8 \times 1.0)}$
$= \sqrt{19.6}$
= 4.4271... m/s (= **4.43 m/s** (to 3 s.f.))
[3 marks for correct answer, otherwise 1 mark for correct rearrangement and 1 mark for correct substitution]

9.4 $F = \frac{\Delta(mv)}{t}$, so $t = \frac{\Delta(mv)}{F}$
Final momentum = 0
so $t = \frac{0 - (30.0 \times 4.4271...)}{266} = 0.49930...$ s (= **0.499 s** (to 3 s.f.))
[2 marks for correct answer, otherwise 1 mark for correct substitution]
You'll get the marks here if you got the answer to 9.3 wrong, as long as your answer is correct for that value, and your method is correct.

9.5 How to grade your answer:
Level 0: There is no relevant information. *[No marks]*
Level 1: There is a suggestion of which material to use, and a brief description of why this is the best choice of material. *[1 to 2 marks]*
Level 2: There is a suggestion of which material to use, supported by a clear description of why this is the best choice of material. *[3 to 4 marks]*
Level 3: There is a suggestion of which material to use, supported by a clear and detailed description of why this is the best choice of material. *[5 to 6 marks]*
Here are some points your answer may include:
Material B should be used.
Material B is the best choice because it compresses the most under a given force.
This means that, of the materials shown, the time taken for a child who falls on it to come to rest will be longest.
Since force is equal to the rate of change of momentum $\left(F = \frac{\Delta(mv)}{t}\right)$, the longer it takes for an object to come to a stop, the lower the force on the object.
So a child will experience a lower force when they fall on material B, and is less likely to be injured.
Material B also deforms elastically.
Which means it will return to its original shape after the force compressing it has been removed.
This means the same spot on the ground will be compressible repeatedly, and can help prevent injury numerous times.

10.1 Coiling a current-carrying wire into a solenoid causes the magnetic fields around each loop to line up with each other and add together *[1 mark]*. This produces a lot of field lines that are pointing in the same direction and close together *[1 mark]*. The closer together field lines are, the stronger the magnetic field, so the magnetic field around and through the coil is stronger than around a straight current-carrying wire *[1 mark]*.

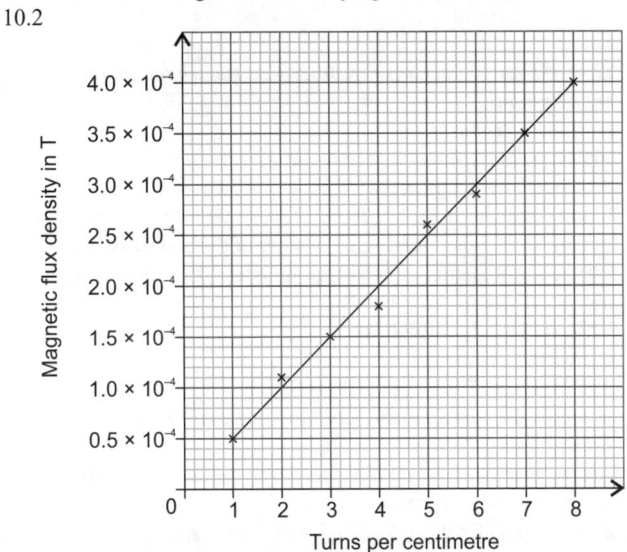

10.2

[1 mark for all points plotted correctly, 1 mark for suitable straight line of best fit]

10.3 The magnetic flux density is proportional to the number of turns per centimetre *[1 mark]*.

10.4 Comparing the equation for magnetic flux density to the equation for a straight line graph, $y = mx + c$,
y = magnetic flux density, x = turns per centimetre, $c = 0$, and $m = \mu \times$ current
m is the gradient, so to find μ, find the gradient and divide by the current.
gradient = $\frac{\text{change in } y}{\text{change in } x} = \frac{4.0 \times 10^{-4} - 0.5 \times 10^{-4}}{8 - 1} = 0.5 \times 10^{-4}$
so μ = gradient ÷ current = (0.5 × 10⁻⁴) ÷ 0.4 = **1.25 × 10⁻⁴**
[3 marks for correct answer, otherwise 1 mark for correct calculation of the gradient and 1 mark for correct method of calculation of μ]

Set B — Paper 1

1.1 230 V *[1 mark]*
1.2 0 A *[1 mark]*. The earth wire only carries current when there is a fault *[1 mark]*.
1.3 electrical power = potential difference × current / $P = VI$ *[1 mark]*
1.4 1.61 kW = 1610 W
$P = VI$
$\Rightarrow I = \dfrac{P}{V} = \dfrac{1610}{230} = \mathbf{7.0\ A}$
[2 marks for correct answer, otherwise 1 mark for correct substitution.]
1.5 thermistor *[1 mark]*
2.1 Elastic potential energy store *[1 mark]*
2.2 dissipated, wasted *[1 mark]*
2.3 E.g. it is transferred to the thermal energy store of the bow/arrow/surroundings / the kinetic energy store of the bow *[1 mark]*
2.4 Efficiency = useful output energy transfer ÷ total input energy transfer *[1 mark]*
2.5 Efficiency = 15 ÷ 20 = 0.75
Convert to a percentage:
0.75 × 100 = **75%**
[2 marks for correct answer, otherwise 1 mark for correct substitution.]
3.1 Kinetic energy = ½ × mass × speed² / $E_k = \tfrac{1}{2}mv^2$ *[1 mark]*
3.2 $m = 58 \div 1000 = 0.058$ kg
$E_k = \tfrac{1}{2} \times 0.058 \times 25^2 = 18.125$ J = **18 J (to 2 s.f.)**
[3 marks for correct answer, otherwise 1 mark for converting the mass of the ball to kg and 1 mark for correct substitution.]
3.3 The ball ends up below where it starts. Therefore, energy has transferred out of its gravitational potential energy store *[1 mark]*. Some of this energy has transferred to its kinetic energy store, causing it to speed up *[1 mark]*.
4.1 E.g. solids tend to be denser than liquids *[1 mark]*.
4.2 E.g. the particles are closer together in solids than in liquids *[1 mark]*. This means there are more particles in a certain volume, giving solids a higher typical density *[1 mark]*.
4.3 Pumice is porous/contains lots of holes, so a large proportion of its volume is occupied by air *[1 mark]*. Air has a very low density, so the average density of the rock is lower than for most other solids *[1 mark]*.
4.4 700 − 500 = **200 cm³** *[1 mark]*
The combined volume of the rock and water is 700 cm³, so the volume of the rock is equal to the water's volume subtracted from this.
4.5 E.g. She could put the water and rock into a beaker/container with more graduations/a higher resolution *[1 mark]*.
4.6 $\rho = m \div V = 420 \div 200 = 2.1$ g/cm³
[2 marks for correct answer, otherwise 1 mark for correct substitution.]
This density suggests the rock could be made from sandstone, which has a stated density of 2.2 g/cm³ in Table 1 *[1 mark]*.
You'd get the marks here even if you got 4.4 wrong, as long as your working and reasoning is correct.
5.1 Both atoms have the same atomic number but different mass numbers *[1 mark]*.
5.2 The mass numbers and atomic numbers on each side of the equation need to balance.
Mass number:
2 + 3 = 4 + A so A = **1** *[1 mark]*
Atomic number:
1 + 1 = 2 + B, so B = **0** *[1 mark]*
5.3 Neutron *[1 mark]*
5.4 Nuclei have a positive electric charge *[1 mark]*, and positive charges repel each other *[1 mark]*. This force gets stronger the closer they are together, so a large force needs to be provided to overcome this repulsion *[1 mark]*.

6.1 Energy is transferred by heating from the water to the surroundings *[1 mark]*. This causes the (average) energy in the kinetic energy stores of the water particles to decrease *[1 mark]*, which means a decrease in temperature.
6.2 Level 0: No relevant content *[No marks]*
Level 1: Simple statements about whether the student's investigation is a fair test. However, the response does not clearly link the validity of the results to flaws in the investigation's method *[1 to 2 marks]*.
Level 2: The results and conclusion are identified as not being valid. Some ways in which the student tried to make their investigation a fair test are identified. The failure to make his experiment a fair test is clearly linked to the validity of the results *[3 to 4 marks]*.
Level 3: A detailed and coherent argument is produced which shows clear and logical progression. There is a detailed discussion on the validity of the results and the student's conclusion, and whether the investigation was a fair test *[5 to 6 marks]*.
Here are some points your answer may include:
The student's conclusion is not valid.
The initial temperature of the water was different when testing insulators A and B.
The student should compare the rate of temperature change from when the water temperature was 70 °C for both insulators.
The water temperature for insulator A drops by 20 °C in around 70 minutes. The water temperature for material B drops by around 25 °C in 70 minutes, and so it has a faster rate of cooling. This means that it is likely that insulator A is the better insulator.
The student tried to ensure the investigation was a fair test, e.g. by keeping the mass of water used the same, the thickness of the insulation used the same, the room temperature the same and the equipment used the same for each insulation tested.
However, because the initial temperatures of the water were not the same for each material tested, the investigation is not a fair test / the results are not valid.
Different initial water temperatures may have affected the rate of cooling of the water.
This means the student cannot draw a meaningful conclusion from his results.
6.3 Wall thickness *[1 mark]* and the thermal conductivity of the wall material *[1 mark]*.

7.1 [LDR circuit symbol] *[1 mark]*

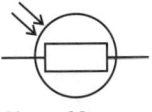

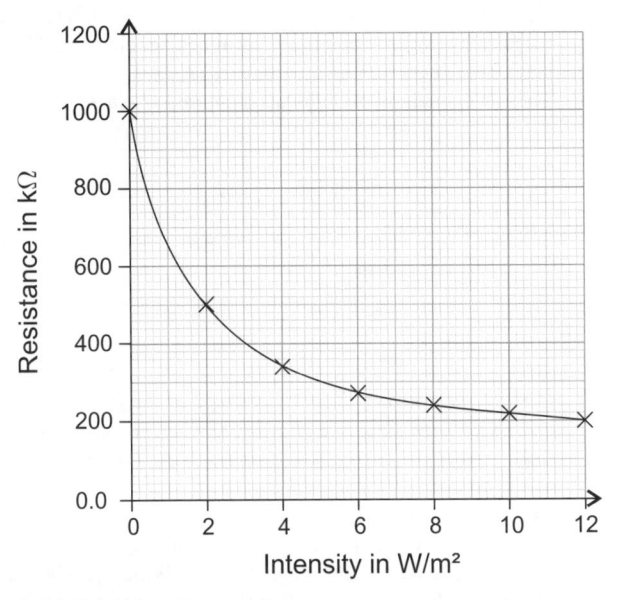

7.2 [Graph: Resistance in kΩ vs Intensity in W/m². Points plotted at approximately (0, 1000), (4, 500), (6, 350), (8, 275), (10, 225), (12, 200) with smooth curve of best fit.]

[1 mark for the two data points plotted correctly and 1 mark for sensible line of best fit.]

7.3 light intensity *[1 mark]*

7.4 As the light intensity increases, the resistance decreases *[1 mark]*. The relationship is non-linear/the resistance decreases at a decreasing rate *[1 mark]*.

7.5 The more sheets of tissue paper between the bulb and the LDR, the less light is able to pass through to the LDR. This means the light intensity incident on the LDR is reduced, so the resistance of the LDR is increased *[1 mark]*.

7.6 E.g. keep the light bulb a constant distance away from the LDR / ensure that the light bulb is always vertically above the LDR / ensure that the light level in the rest of the room is kept constant *[1 mark]*.

7.7 Thickness = 0.13 mm *[1 mark]*

7.8 E.g. The sensitivity is too low *[1 mark]* so the output would remain the same (or be very similar) for different thicknesses of paper *[1 mark]*.

7.9 E.g. the thickness measurements are only valid for white tissue paper / the thickness measurements may be inaccurate / the material/quality of the tissue paper may also affect the amount of light transmitted *[1 mark]*.

8.1 The pushing force on the plunger does work to compress the air *[1 mark]*. The energy transferred to the air increases its internal energy and its temperature so that the char cloth ignites *[1 mark]*.

8.2 The particles get faster / their average speed increases *[1 mark]*.

8.3 Level 0: No relevant content *[0 marks]*
Level 1: Simple statements are made about pressure and temperature, but the response does not clearly link these to ideas about particles or the char cloth burning and transferring energy. *[1 to 2 marks]*
Level 2: The response attempts to explain why the pressure increases because of a temperature increase. The explanation is linked to the motion of particles and energy transfer from the char cloth burning, but there are some errors or omissions in the explanation *[3 to 4 marks]*
Level 3: A clear explanation of why both the temperature and pressure increases. The response explains how the burning char cloth leads to an increased temperature, how the motion of particles leads to pressure and why the pressure increases when the particles move faster *[5 to 6 marks]*

Here are some points your answer may include:
Energy is transferring from the chemical energy store of the char cloth to the thermal energy store of the air as the char cloth burns.
So the energy in the kinetic energy stores of the air particles increases, and the temperature increases.
Since the temperature increases and the volume is kept constant, the pressure also increases.
When the air particles collide with the wall they exert a force on the wall.
This force causes a pressure.
As the temperature increases, the speed of the particles increases.
This means they collide with the walls with a larger force.
They also collide with the walls more frequently.
This leads to an increase in the pressure.

9.1 $I = 40 \div 1000 = 0.04$ A
$R = V \div I = 6.0 \div 0.04 = $ **150 Ω**
[3 marks for correct answer, otherwise 1 mark for converting the current and 1 mark for correct substitution.]

9.2 Resistance of lamp + 10 Ω = 150 Ω
⇒ Resistance of lamp = 150 – 10 = **140 Ω** *[1 mark]*

9.3 $I = 30 \div 1000 = 0.03$ A
Total resistance = $V \div I = 6.0 \div 0.03 = 200$ Ω
Resistance of lamp
= total resistance – resistance of variable resistor
= 200 – 100 = **100 Ω**
[2 marks for correct answer, otherwise 1 mark for calculating the total resistance in the circuit.]

9.4 There is less current through/p.d. across the lamp *[1 mark]*, so the lamp is dimmer *[1 mark]*. This means that the filament is cooler, so it has a smaller resistance *[1 mark]*.

12

10.1 change in thermal energy
= mass × specific heat capacity × temperature change
= 2.0 × 4200 × (100 – 20) = **672 000 J**
[2 marks for correct answer, otherwise 1 mark for correct substitution.]

10.2 Time = 5.6 minutes = 5.6 × 60 s = 336 s
$P = E \div t = 672\,000 \div 336 =$ **2000 W**
[3 marks for correct answer, otherwise 1 mark for converting time to seconds and 1 mark for correct substitution.]

10.3 Mass that changes state = 2.0 – 1.8 = 0.2 kg
Time heater takes boiling the water = 10 – 5.6
= 4.4 minutes = 264 s
Energy = power × time
So heater transfers 2000 × 264 = 528 000 J of energy
Energy for change of state = mass × specific latent heat
So specific latent heat = energy ÷ mass
= 528 000 ÷ 0.2 = **2 640 000 J/kg**
[5 marks for correct answer, otherwise 1 mark for calculating the mass that changes state, 1 mark for calculating the time taken for the heater to boil the water, 1 mark for calculating the energy transferred by the heater and 1 mark for correct substitution into E = mL.]

10.4 Some of the energy is transferred to the surroundings rather than the water *[1 mark]*. This means that the value used for energy is higher than that used to change the water's state of matter *[1 mark]*.

11.1 It will gain (two) neutrons *[1 mark]*. The fission reaction releases neutrons *[1 mark]* that are absorbed by the carbon-12 nucleus *[1 mark]*.

11.2 One half-life is the time taken for 50% of the carbon-14 to decay. From the graph, this is 5700 years.
So 11 400 years is 2 half-lives *[1 mark]*.
Therefore, the amount remaining halves and halves again to become a quarter of the original amount.
So the fraction is ¼ *[1 mark]*.

11.3 The diamond may absorb some of the radiation emitted by the carbon-14, and so reduce the amount of irradiation *[1 mark]*. The carbon-14 is encased in the diamond and cannot come into direct contact with a person / rub off on them. This helps reduce the risk of contamination *[1 mark]*.

11.4 $E = Q \times V$
$Q = E \div V = 2.7 \times 10^3 \div 2.0 = 1350$ GC = **1.35 TC**
[2 marks for correct answer, otherwise 1 mark for correct substitution or a correct answer given in incorrect units]

11.5 The half-life is very long / the battery will be used for a very long time. The casing needs to last a long time in order to protect future generations from being contaminated/irradiated *[1 mark]*.

11.6 Advantage: Any one from, e.g. lasts a long time so no need to replace / helps to deal with the disposal of nuclear waste / energy is already available so no further use of energy resources *[1 mark]*.
Disadvantage: Any one from, e.g. insides are radioactive, which can cause harm / expensive to produce / can only deliver a tiny current *[1 mark]*.

Set B — Paper 2

1.1 $(1.8 \times 10^{32}) \div (2.0 \times 10^{30}) =$ **90** *[1 mark]*
1.2 Any two from: e.g. Eta Carinae A is surrounded by a cloud of gas and dust so is difficult to measure / Eta Carinae A is very far away / you can't measure the mass directly *[2 marks — 1 mark for each correct suggestion]*.
1.3 Nuclear fusion *[1 mark]* is the process by which lighter elements (such as hydrogen) combine to form heavier elements *[1 mark]*.
1.4 black hole *[1 mark]* and neutron star *[1 mark]*
1.5 The wavelength of the light has increased *[1 mark]*.
2.1

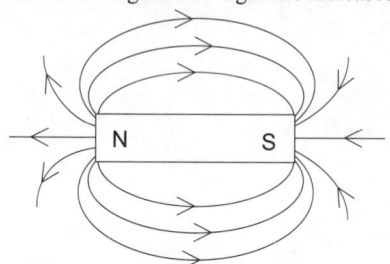

[1 mark for drawing the correct shape of the field, 1 mark for arrows on each field line showing the correct direction of the field, 1 mark for correctly drawing at least 3 lines at each pole which do not touch each other.]

2.2 At the poles / at a pole *[1 mark]*.
2.3 Iron is a magnetic material, so it turns into an induced magnet when it is placed into the magnetic field *[1 mark]*. The side of the iron closest to the north pole of the magnet becomes a south pole, so the two attract each other / the force between a permanent and induced magnet is always attractive *[1 mark]*.
2.4 Work done = force × distance / $W = Fs$ *[1 mark]*
2.5 15 cm = 15 ÷ 100 = 0.15 m
Work done = 0.80 × 0.15
= **0.12 J**
[2 marks for correct answer, otherwise 1 mark for correct substitution.]
2.6 It feels a force of attraction towards the south pole *[1 mark]*.
2.7 A primary coil and a secondary coil *[1 mark]* wound around an iron core *[1 mark]*.
2.8 Step-up transformers have less turns on the primary coil than the secondary coil ($n_p < n_s$), whereas for step-down transformers, $n_p > n_s$ *[1 mark]*. The function of step-up transformers is to increase the potential difference ($V_p < V_s$), whereas step-down transformers decrease the potential difference ($V_p > V_s$) *[1 mark]*.

AQA GCSE Physics / PAHP241 / Answer Book

© CGP 2017 — copying more than 5% of this booklet is not permitted

3.1 How to grade your answer:
Level 0: There is no relevant information. *[No marks]*
Level 1: There is a brief method described, but significant detail is missing / there is no mention of how to ensure measurements taken are accurate.
[1 to 2 marks]
Level 2: A method is described, but some detail might be missing. Answer includes at least one way of ensuring accurate measurements are taken. *[3 to 4 marks]*
Level 3: There is a clear, detailed and logical method given, including effective ways to ensure accuracy.
[5 to 6 marks]
Here are some points your answer may include:
Set the frequency of the ripples using the signal generator.
Lay a ruler alongside the shadows of the ripples on the screen below the ripple tank.
Use the ruler to measure the wavelength of the ripples.
To get a more accurate wavelength, measure the distance between several ripples and divide by the number of complete waves to work out the average wavelength. The more waves that are measured over, the greater the accuracy of this average wavelength.
Alternatively you could place the ruler by the side of the ripples and take a photograph of the ripples and the ruler. The wavelength of the ripples can then be measured using the ruler in the photograph for scale.
In a photo, the ripples will be stationary as you measure them, so you should be able to get a more accurate distance measurement than if trying to measure moving waves.
To try to get an accurate result, it is also important to make sure that distance measurements are taken from directly overhead (to reduce parallax error).
Use the formula $v = f\lambda$ to calculate the speed of the waves.

3.2 E.g. signal generator frequency / the depth of water the dipper moves through to generate the waves / the temperature of the water *[1 mark]*.

3.3 Speed in m/s

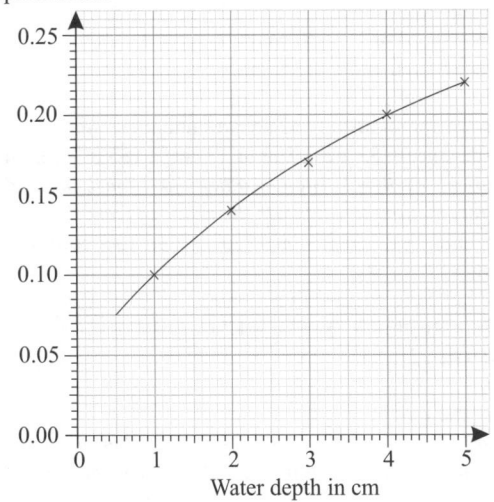

[1 mark for plotting both data points correctly, 1 mark for drawing a sensible curve of best fit.]

3.4 As the depth increases, the speed increases *[1 mark]*.
The relationship is non-linear / speed increases at a decreasing rate *[1 mark]*.

4.1 The water in the white teapot cools down more slowly than the water in the black teapot *[1 mark]*. The teapots cool down because energy is mostly transferred away from the surface by infrared radiation *[1 mark]*. Black surfaces are better emitters of infrared radiation than white surfaces *[1 mark]*. So energy is transferred away at a faster rate by the black teapot at any given temperature *[1 mark]*.

4.2 Each teapot is absorbing radiation at the same rate as it is emitting it *[1 mark]*.

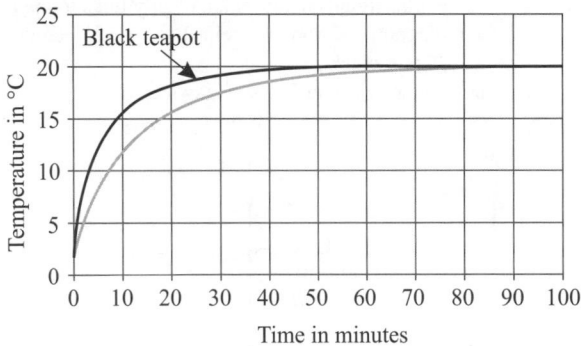

4.3

[1 mark for line starting at 2 °C, 1 mark for line drawn reaching 20 °C more quickly than for the white teapot, 1 mark for line levelling off at 20 °C.]

4.4 An object that absorbs all radiation incident on it / an object that does not reflect or transmit any radiation *[1 mark]*.

5.1 The arrows represent the direction the football is travelling in *[1 mark]*. Speed is a scalar quantity. It doesn't need arrows because it has no direction *[1 mark]*.

5.2 Displacement = 0 m *[1 mark]*
Displacement is a vector between the start and end point of the path. Here, the start and end points are the same, so the overall displacement of the football is 0 m.

5.3 Average acceleration = change in velocity ÷ time taken / $a = \dfrac{\Delta v}{t}$ *[1 mark]*

5.4 Change in velocity = 5 + 3 = 8 m/s
Average acceleration = 8 ÷ 0.2 = **40 m/s²**
[2 marks for correct answer, otherwise 1 mark for correct substitution.]

5.5 $F = ma$
Mass of ball = 400 ÷ 1000 = 0.4 kg
So average force = 0.4 × 40 = **16 N**
[3 marks for correct answer, otherwise 1 mark for converting the ball's mass to kg and 1 mark for correct substitution.]

6.1 convex/converging *[1 mark]*

6.2 Magnification = $\dfrac{\text{image height}}{\text{object height}}$
So magnification = gradient = $\dfrac{9.2 - 0.8}{2.85 - 0.25}$
= 3.23... = **3.2 (to 2 s.f.)**
[3 marks for correct answer, otherwise 1 mark for correct substitution into equation of a gradient with valid data from the graph, 1 mark for either a correct unrounded answer OR an incorrect answer correctly rounded to two significant figures.]

6.3 Level 0: There is no relevant information. *[No marks]*
Level 1: Some aspects of the ray diagram are correct. An explanation is made which attempts to answer the question. *[1 to 2 marks]*
Level 2: The ray diagram is mostly correct. An explanation is made which attempts to link the ray diagram to how this helps nearsighted people. Most of the points made in the explanation are correct. *[3 to 4 marks]*
Level 3: The ray diagram is correct. A coherent and logical explanation is made which clearly links to the ray diagram and how this helps nearsighted people. *[5 to 6 marks]*

Here are some points your answer may include:

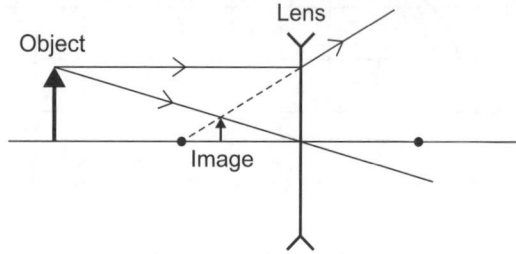

[Ray diagram showing Object, Lens (concave), and Image]

The ray diagram shows that the concave lens forms a virtual image of the object.
The ray diagram also shows that the image is closer to the lens than the object.
The image is also the correct way up.
Therefore, anyone looking through the lens will see the image of the object nearer than it is.
Nearsighted people will see this image more clearly than the object which is further away.

7.1 refraction *[1 mark]*
7.2 E.g. don't shine the laser into their/the students' eyes / turn the laser off when it is not in use *[1 mark]*.
7.3 E.g.

[Diagram of wavefronts entering a block with smaller gaps between the wavefronts in the block]

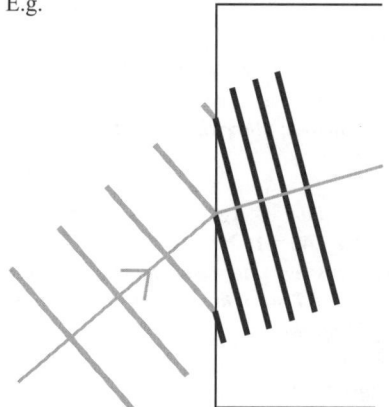

[1 mark for at least three wave fronts drawn in the correct direction in the block, 1 mark for smaller gaps drawn between the wave fronts in the block.]

7.4 The frequency of the laser light stays the same *[1 mark]*.
7.5 $v = f\lambda$
Rearranging: $f_{in} = v_{in} \div \lambda_{in}$ and $f_{out} = v_{out} \div \lambda_{out}$
The frequency does not change during refraction, so $f_{in} = f_{out}$.
$\frac{v_{in}}{\lambda_{in}} = \frac{v_{out}}{\lambda_{out}}$, so $\lambda_{in} = \frac{v_{in} \times \lambda_{out}}{v_{out}}$
$\lambda_{in} = \frac{(2.0 \times 10^8)(7.0 \times 10^{-7})}{3.0 \times 10^8}$
$\lambda_{in} = 4.66... \times 10^{-7}$ m $(= 4.7 \times 10^{-7}$ m (to 2 s.f.))
[4 marks for correct answer, otherwise 1 mark for equating $\frac{v_{in}}{\lambda_{in}}$ and $\frac{v_{out}}{\lambda_{out}}$, 1 mark for correct rearrangement to get an expression for λ_{in} and 1 mark for correct substitution.]
An alternative method is to realise that since the two frequencies are equal, $\frac{v_{in}}{v_{out}} = \frac{\lambda_{in}}{\lambda_{out}}$, so the wavelength inside the block is $= \frac{2}{3} \lambda_{out}$.

8.1 980 N *[1 mark]*
Because the cube floats, the upthrust must be equal to its weight.
8.2

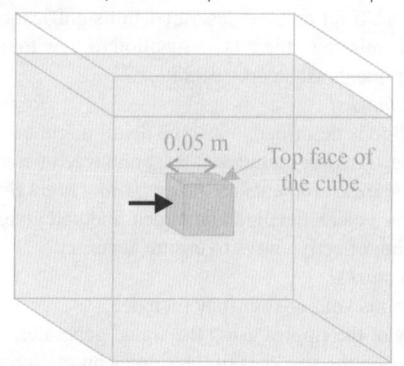

[Diagram of cube in water with arrow pointing right on the left face, labelled 0.05 m and "Top face of the cube"]

[1 mark for arrow pointing right on the left-hand side of the cube at right angles to the face, accept if tail of the arrow starts from the left-hand side of the cube and the arrow goes into the cube.]
A fluid exerts a force at right angles to any surface in contact with the fluid.

8.3 Area of the top face $= 0.05 \times 0.05 = 2.5 \times 10^{-3}$ m^2
$F = p \times A = 1470 \times 2.5 \times 10^{-3} = $ **3.675 N (= 3.7 N (to 2 s.f.))**
[3 marks for correct answer, otherwise 1 mark for correctly calculating the area, 1 mark for correct substitution.]

8.4 $p = h\rho g$
Height of the water column $= \frac{p}{\rho \times g} = \frac{1470}{1000 \times 9.8}$
$= $ **0.15 m**
[2 marks for correct answer, otherwise 1 mark for correct substitution.]

8.5 The bottom of the cube is at a greater depth than the top. As pressure increases with depth, the bottom experiences a greater pressure *[1 mark]*. The force applied is proportional to the pressure, so the force acting is greater at the bottom of the cube *[1 mark]*.

9.1 Between 0 and 10 s, the player uniformly accelerates from 0 to 4 m/s *[1 mark]*. From 10 to 35 s, they decelerate (at an increasing rate) *[1 mark]*. From 35 to 60 s, they move with a constant speed of 2 m/s *[1 mark]*.
Distance = area under the graph.
Each graph square $= 1 \times 5 = 5$ m.
There are approximately 32 squares under the graph line.
Total distance $= 32 \times 5 = $ **160 m (Accept 155 m - 165 m)**
[2 marks for correct distance, otherwise 1 mark for evidence of a correct method to calculate the distance from the graph]

9.2 Momentum before collision = momentum after collision
$p = mv$
Let right be the positive direction:
$\Rightarrow (70 \times 9) - (56 \times 7) = (56 \times 1.5) + (70 \times v)$
$\Rightarrow 630 - 392 = 84 + 70v$
$\Rightarrow 70v = 154$
$\Rightarrow v = $ **2.2 m/s**
[4 marks for calculating correct answer, otherwise 1 mark for stating that momentum is conserved, 1 mark for correct substitutions, 1 mark for rearranging for v.]

9.3

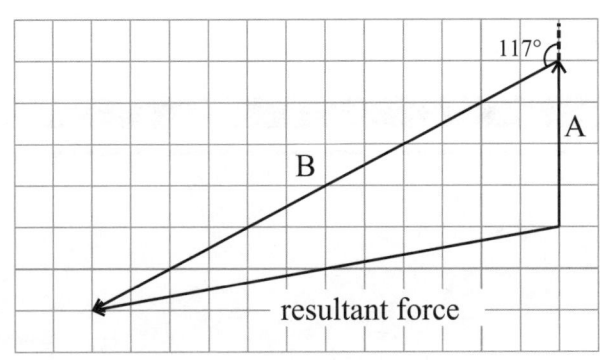

Length of resultant force arrow = 12.1 cm = 12.1 squares
The scale is 1 square = 5 N so the resultant force
= 5 × 12.1 = **60.5 N**
[3 marks for correct answer (anywhere between 59.5 and 61.5 N), otherwise award up to 2 marks: 1 mark for arrows drawn to the correct length, 1 mark for drawing B at the correct angle to A, 1 mark for arrows correctly drawn to show resultant force, 1 mark for giving the length of the resultant force arrow.]

10.1 When the child is down towards the floor the spring is stretched. The stretched spring exerts a force downwards (causing a clockwise moment) which brings the child back up again *[1 mark]*.
When the child is up high, the spring is compressed.
The compressed spring exerts a force upwards (causing an anticlockwise moment) which helps to bring the child back down again *[1 mark]*.

10.2 Moment produced by spring to balance child's moment
= 150 Nm
Moment = force × perpendicular distance / $M = Fd$
Force of spring = $M \div d$ = 150 ÷ 0.20 = 750 N
Force = spring constant × extension / $F = ke$
$k = F \div e$ = 750 ÷ 0.15 = **5000 N/m**
[4 marks for correct answer, otherwise 1 mark for correct substitution into $F = M \div d$, 1 mark for correctly calculating the force, 1 mark for correct substitution into $F = ke$.]

10.3 $E_e = \frac{1}{2}ke^2 \Rightarrow e = \sqrt{\frac{2E_e}{k}} = \sqrt{\frac{2 \times 225}{5000}} = $ **0.30 m**
[3 marks for calculating the correct answer, otherwise 1 mark for correctly rearranging the formula, 1 mark for correct substitution.]

www.cgpbooks.co.uk